'Miss Teach'

A Memoir Handwritten with Love
by Anne I. Remis

*Dedicated to all of my students
and especially to the memory
of Andrea Levy*

Library of Congress Control Number 2004100531

Remis, Anne I.

Miss Teach
A Teacher's Memoir Handwritten with Love

A pioneer Rochester teacher in the field of education for children with disabilities recalls the personal joys and challenges of that not-so-long ago time when
such education was in its infancy.

1. Remis, Anne I., 1914-   , Biography - Teaching
2. Remis, Anne I., 1914-   , Biography - Children with disabilities

 ISBN: 0-9748866-0-2

'Miss Teach'

A Memoir
Handwritten with Love
by Anne I. Remis

Foreword by Winifred Fletcher

Introduction by
Elizabeth Joy Howard

Transcribed and edited by Anne H. Howard

Designed and edited by Dennis M. Howard

All royalties from the sale of this book
will go for the benefit of handicapped children
through CP Rochester, Rochester, NY 14623

Website: *http://www.missteach.org*
Email: *mail@missteach.org*

Published by
The Movement for a Better America, Inc.
PO Box 470
Mt. Freedom, NJ   07970

"Now is the winter of our discontent
Made glorious summer by this Sun of York;
.....But I that am not shaped for sportive tricks
Nor made to court an amorous looking glass,
I that am rudely stamped and want Love's majesty
To strut before a wanton ambling nymph;
I that am curtailed of this fair proportion,
Cheated of feature by dissembling Nature,
Deformed, unfinished, sent before my time
Into this breathing world, scarce half made up,
And that so lamely and unfashionable
That dogs bark at me as I halt by them -
Why I in this weak piping time of peace,
Have no delight to pass away the time,
Unless to see my shadow in the sun
And descant on mine own deformity."

Richard III, Act 1, Scene 1, William Shakespeare

Foreword

Partners in Progress

by Winifred Fletcher

How do you write a foreword to a memoir written by a great and wonderful friend you have known for fifty years?

Anne Remis and I both began working with physically handicapped children at the same time -- she as a teacher of school-aged children and I as a preschool teacher.

Later, I became director of a clinic for treatment and training of children with disabilities. It was the early 1950's and treatment and education of such children was still in its infancy.

What gave the movement impetus were dedicated parents who had finally come together to found organizations that became powerful advocates for medical research and education in this new field. Their objective was to make proper schooling available for children with all degrees of handicap.

The result was that medicine and education became partners. Our clinic was a treatment center and a training ground for the public schools, while the schools pioneered innovative ways to educate children to their full potential without regard to their degree of disability.

In these pages, Anne Remis has given a detailed account of how one teacher resolved the many problems facing such an educator -- at times by sheer ingenuity, and at times by clear-headed application of the principles of education she had herself learned in Teacher's College. The result is a valuable resource for today's young teachers.

Many new inventions and assistive devices have been developed over the intervening years, but nothing can replace the value of a teacher's honest dedication, diligence, and ingenuity in developing ever new ways to help children overcome handicaps and reach their full educational potential. Indeed, without such commitment and dedication on the part of many others, few of these fantastic technical developments would have been invented.

So read this book and laugh and cry and wonder as I did, and become aware of what empathy and knowledge and love can do to resolve the complex needs of these fascinating children.

Winifred Fletcher
June 30, 2002

Acknowledgements

My thanks to all who helped in the preparation of this book including my many nieces and nephews who read the manuscript and encouraged me to carry on -- especially Liz Pryor and Anne Mary Colgan. Thanks, too, to my household aides whose caring assistance made life easier.

Thanks also to Wynn Fletcher, who wrote the generous foreword, and to my grand-niece, Elizabeth Joy Howard, for her insightful introduction. She is now pursuing her own path teaching 11th and 12th grade English on the Navajo Reservation in Newcomb, N.M. Finally, my gratitude to my niece, Anne Howard, who transcribed and edited my lengthy handscripts, and to her husband Dennis, who brought his long experience in journalism and communications to designing and editing this book. For all who have helped, this has been a labor of love.   *Anne I. Remis*

Introduction

A Teacher's Identity

By Elizabeth Howard

As a culture and as individuals, we tend to underestimate the contribution stories make to our collective and individual identity, oral stories in particular. It is only recently that I came to fully appreciate how many of the stories I was told as a child informed and affected my sense of self. They may very well be the reason that I became a teacher.

My teaching license is in language arts, but for my first two years in teaching, I worked as a special education para-professional. In that short time, my experiences ranged from working with a profoundly mentally challenged boy to working with students with learning disabilities as well as with students in their early teens who have emotional and behavioral problems.

There are days, of course, when I wonder whatever possessed me to enter this field. That's when I remember the stories that I heard from my mother about her Aunt Anne as I was growing up. Anne Remis is my great aunt on my mother's side. Some of the stories I heard about her, no doubt, sunk deep into my young brain and had at least some influence on my career choice. Now, these stories have been written down.

A familiar phrase in special education is that children with disabilities are "like some, like all, like no other" children. The same can be said for the teachers who educate these children. The stories contained in this book tell us about who we are, who we were, and who we are becoming as professionals. They add to and strengthen our identity.

One of these stories tells about developing and using a communication board to help students without speech to better express themselves. When I was working with my severe needs student, we used very similar devices. The technology may be further advanced, but the need and purpose is the same.

Helping students to communicate goes much deeper than technology. The students I worked with were all capable of speaking. What was difficult for them was communicating without swearing, raising their voices, or using sarcasm. So I still had to teach my students how to communicate. Teaching a student with Angelman's syndrome is essentially the same thing Anne Remis did with her students. Teaching communication skills is a crucial part of any teacher's job.

A good example is the story Anne shares about what she had to do in order to help her students see a flock of beautiful red birds sitting in a snowy tree. It illustrates another goal that all teachers strive to help their students reach: a deeper appreciation of the simple beauties of life.

This is important because many students often do not see much, if any, beauty in the world. Many of them come from abusive households where physical and verbal fights are an everyday occurrence and where there is no food in the house because last week's paycheck was spent on alcohol and drugs.

It is difficult for these kids to see that there is love and beauty in the world just outside their window. My job, and the job of all teachers, is to lift them up to see. This book will encourage us to remember that.

Perhaps the most important lesson a teacher can teach is the lesson of dignity and respect that is woven throughout these stories. A special education teacher must be extremely careful to honor the dignity of her students and to respect them as individuals. We also have to teach them to respect themselves and others.

It can be very difficult for a person with one or more disabilities to have respect for himself. The teacher's job is to encourage self-respect by always treating the student respectfully, whether or not that student shows respect in return.

The special education teacher also models for others how a person with disabilities ought to be treated. Quite often students with disabilities are horribly teased and made fun of by their "typical" peers. Sadly, they are not always aware that they are being abused and end up internalizing the attitudes of their abusers. And even when they are aware, many cannot stand up for themselves. The teacher's role in advocating for her students and modeling dignity and respect becomes even more critical in these situations.

If we are to impart these messages to our students, we must all strive to be "like some, like all, like no other" teacher. Good teachers must be people of strength, courage and integrity.

The stories in this book inspire us to do just that. They exemplify the qualities of effective communication, dignity, respect, and the ability to find beauty in difficult situations. In reading them, my identity is enriched and my confidence strengthened. They make me proud of my heritage, both personal and professional.

Hopefully, the stories in this book will give all of those who read them the same sense of pride and purpose that we must all strive to pass on to our students.

And, who knows, somewhere out there may be another young person seeking his or her calling who may be so affected by this book as to walk in the author's footsteps. For young people like that, these stories will remain an inspiration.

Since writing this, I have moved on to a challenging new assignment teaching 11th and 12th grade English classes at a high school on the Navajo reservation in the northwest corner of New Mexico. For all of the reasons I have stated above, I feel fortunate to take with me all of the lessons I have learned from this book.

Handwritten with Love

IRETIRED FROM TEACHING IN 1978, after research, study and teaching children with cerebral palsy and then working in public school special classes for 27 years. At this point, I feel almost a moral commitment to share my thoughts on the education of all children. There will be no fiction or hypothetical anecdotes in my story. All that follows is handwritten with love.

I grew up in Clinton, a small town in upstate New York that prospered during the canal building days in the early 19th century. The surrounding area is rich in history dating back to the French and Indian wars a century earlier, but Clinton itself was founded by pioneers from Connecticut in 1787. The town was named for George Clinton, a popular Revolutionary War political leader, who was elected seven times as governor of the State of New York. He was also twice elected as Vice President under Thomas Jefferson and James Madison.

Serving as home to several outstanding academies and seminaries, the town became famous for its schools. Hamilton College is the most notable, founded as an academy in 1793 and becoming chartered as a college about 20 years later. Our family home on College Street had been a Hamilton College student residence for years before my parents acquired it in the early 1920's, so you might say our roots ran deep in the academic history of Clinton.

My parents were recent immigrants from central Europe with all the aspirations that sociologists have come to ascribe to this group. There were six children. I was in the middle, a sister and two brothers before me and two brothers who arrived later. Before we moved to

Clinton, our family lived in Bayonne, N.J., but work was hard to find in Bayonne and life was a struggle for a family with three children and the prospect of more on the way. So my parents picked up stakes and moved to Clinton on the strength of rumors that work was plentiful there. In fact, that proved to be not quite true, compounded as it was by a measure of discrimination against newcomers by residents who had built the town a century earlier. I grew up knowing what it meant to be a child from a poor family surrounded by more affluent neighbors. Nevertheless, we survived on the strength of my mother's thrift and industry and my father's willingness to take on any honest work that could feed his growing family.

My mother worked as a housekeeper at the College and took in faculty laundry and mending until she managed to save enough to buy the house on College Street. My father, who worked as a "jack-of-all-trades" handyman, pitched in with repairs to overcome the considerable wear and tear from decades of use as a student residence and later as a fraternity house. They planted a vegetable garden in back along with some fruit trees, and we raised our own chickens, too. That meant chores for all of us from the time we were very young.

I was registered in first grade at age 6. School was warm and safe. I don't recall the face of my teacher, Miss Powell, nor can I clearly remember the other children in my class. Being a little one, I can only recall seeing not much above Miss Powell's knees, and that she wore a dark blue serge suit exactly like my mother's. They say I looked like the original Raggedy Anne. I don't remember learning anything, but I knew who, where and why I was there – my mother's angel love. What a wonderful start!

The second grade defined my subsequent school experience in that I wanted love, understanding, patience and beauty and felt that some day I would receive it. Then I would give it back, a truly adult objective for a 7-year-old.

When the rich little girls wore jewelry, I was happy for them but found refuge in my own short-lived defense. I announced that I had a bracelet at home ringed with diamonds, but I was not allowed to wear it because "it hurt people's eyes." Far-fetched as that sounded, the other kids believed me. They were so impressed their eyebrows were practically in their hair.

I also remember the school nurse coming in each morning and asking the class "How many of you had milk for breakfast?" All hands were raised except mine and I overheard her say to my teacher, "No wonder she's so thin and small."

She couldn't know that my angel-mother made the six of us a large pitcher of drink every morning consisting of hot water, a can of Red Cross Condensed Milk, and two tablespoons of her coffee. We called it "coffee" and hadn't the slightest idea we were missing out on anything. However, I was crushed to be labeled "different" and it made a lasting impression on me to be called thin and small.

If you were to see a class picture in the 1920's, you could probably pick me out as the dark eyed, dark haired child with the Buster Brown haircut. Having four brothers at home, I felt comfortable playing with boys in the backyard. We played what we called "knife," which involved using an open jackknife, placed on the back of the hand and flipping it over to try and land it knife-first in the ground. Being a bit of a tomboy, I became quite good at it.

We never had a car, so we didn't even know there was a Clark Mills, New York, just 3 miles away, or Utica a few miles beyond. My small world revolved around our family and relatives and school and work.

When I was 10, my sister and I started doing housework at professors' homes around the campus of Hamilton College where our mother worked. Among my treasured keepsakes, I have letters dated 1935 in which Professor C. Lewis wrote to me and stated, "Your mother is one of the finest women I have ever known." A family of six in the Depression years needed guidance. She filled that need by word and by example. Our lives were normal and poor. We didn't feel disadvantaged.

My mother had attended school in New Jersey for one year in the 3rd grade and learned to read, write and speak English. She wrote phonetically but her ideals and values were straight and true. She never felt deprived. She felt confident and empowered.

I have to admit I had difficulty learning in school. In class, I often didn't know what was being discussed, perhaps because I felt tired or hungry. In some classes, teachers didn't teach the whole lesson because many pupils had prior knowledge and didn't need help . . . or had more experience because their lifestyle was richer . . . or had time and opportunity to read at home. Being poor, we had to work so much of the time, there was little time to study at all, and not much time for parties. I couldn't belong to school organizations, the Glee Club, or drama groups.

I rediscovered these gaps in my education when I started to teach and filled out my learning as I taught.

My oldest brother John, who was a great teacher in common sense matters, taught me to drive a car and gave me an example of his common sense approach. I was surprised by his statement of our first objective, but there are a lot of drivers today who could benefit from his original approach: "First, you learn how to *stop* the engine, *not* how to start it. That way, you will know right off how to keep the car from running all over the place and doing all kinds of damage."

That was my life during this period. I just worked, went to school, and loved every bit of it in an exciting kind of way. Clinton's middle class families were not "our group." We mingled with the very brilliant, educated, well-mannered college professors and their cultured wives by way of employment, or we got to know the very poor. I had many friends in high school, but couldn't enjoy the friendship of the "rich" kids in town.

In grade school or high school, I never had an inkling that my profession would be teaching, and certainly not in a special field for disabled children – which was barely in view at the time. No doubt our family's close association with Hamilton College must have had some influence on my future direction. Since there were only one or two recognizably handicapped children in our whole town, disability went unrecognized as an educational challenge. Children with disabilities either learned along with everyone else or stayed home under their parents' care. I recall one mother who pushed her child around town in a stroller for 8 years. Her girl must have had polio. This child was blessed with a good education, thanks to her mother, and grew up as a happy and loved person.

After high school graduation, baby-sitting became my part-time occupation. The girl next door suggested that I go to Oswego State Normal School (what is now called the New York State University College at Oswego) for three years by working for room and board for a lady she knew. I immediately wrote to Oswego but did not have all the requisite courses I needed for acceptance. But then I learned that I could be accepted as long as I maintained good grades of A or slightly less. This was 1933, when three years of college was all that was required. I was accepted and made the grades.

I graduated in 1935 in the middle of the Great Depression, and at the time there were few positions of any kind to be found after graduation. It never phased me. I didn't feel that poor, since I grew up accustomed to being "without." If I had grown up spoiled rotten, it would have been an emotional disaster for me.

As luck would have it, I was at home for just one week in September of that year when I was offered my first teaching position. My town was centralizing all of its country schools, the famous "little red school houses," and were sending all but the first to fourth grades (a great loss) to the new centralized schools. As a result, the country school where I was hired had just one student – a 10 year-old boy whose brothers and sisters all had left to go to the newer, bigger schools. When I arrived at the school over the hills, he was there all alone and crying bitterly. I tried desperately to help him for one week until finally the School Board made an exception in his case and let him go to the Central School. Suddenly I was without a job again. I went home, but in a few days another offer came, without even a request or knowledge of the school where I had been working. It was a mystery how they even knew of me.

This opportunity was a happy one, my happiest one ever, and opened more doors for me. My new job was in a regional center for the developmentally handicapped for all age levels. My responsibility was to care for young adults using every possible therapy, as well as providing their education. It was a new niche for me, a position particularly suitable for my interest in educating the whole person. It involved music, dancing, drama, academics for each level of student, freedom to do right and good, and an opportunity for great friendships, which I still cherish after over 70 years.

These were great pioneer days in all areas of education. Language, however, was already beginning to lose some of its original meaning. For example, the word "retarded" in the beginning meant that if a student had a broken leg for a period of time, he would lose school time and was, therefore, being "retarded," i.e., slowed up or delayed. However, after a period of time back to school, he would catch up and be returned to "normal." Over time, the word gradually changed to signify mental deficiency.

Sadly, after two and half years, I contracted an illness which forced me to abandon normal activity, including my chosen work, and to retire to bed rest for the next ten years. I have written about this experience in a chapter in a wonderful book called *"Portrait of Healing"* authored by Victoria Rinehart, Ph.D., RN, CNAA, who is on the nursing faculty of the State University of New York Institute of Technology in Rome, N.Y. *(North Country Books, Utica, N.Y. 2002).*

Victoria's book is the story of the people and history of the world famous Trudeau Sanatorium in Saranac Lake, N.Y., originally founded by Dr. Edward L. Trudeau as the Adirondack Cottage Sanatarium between 1873, when Dr. Trudeau first went there for his own recovery, and 1884 when he welcomed his first patients for treatment.

I arrived at Trudeau in 1939 and stayed for nearly ten years until I left for further rehabilitation. It was a memorable decade spent in rest, prayer, and study during which I also got to know many interesting people who were also patients there. They included a Russian princess, several Cuban doctors, and some members of the Czechoslovakian government who fled Europe when Hitler invaded Prague at the onset of World War II.

No doubt my years at Trudeau were also deeply formative for the work I was eventually called to do. I didn't realize it then, but the wonderful care I received from the nurses and doctors there was something I could eventually pass on to others through my work as a teacher of children with disabilities.

The experience was not without its humorous moments. Chief among them was the experience I had when I was sent to New York for further rehabilitation. I was traveling in style in my own Pullman car, when the train stopped to change cars on a railroad siding in Clear Lake, N.Y., and the Pullman car – with me in it – was left abandoned on the siding after the train had left. I had become so used to lying patiently in bed at Trudeau that it never occurred to me to question the fact that the train had not moved for a whole 24 hours.

Fortunately, someone soon discovered the mistake, and I was delivered safe and sound the next evening to Grand Central Station in New York. The patience I learned at Trudeau certainly helped me through that experience, and no doubt came in handy years later during my career as a teacher.

I can never thank my family enough for their loving faith in me, especially my angel mother. So many of her maxims and so much of her example have sustained me and guided my steps. And I will never forget my 8th grade teacher, Bessie Griffin, whom I have written about in my story. She loved music and poetry. Even now, I find myself saying about my pain (with apologies to Emily Dickinson), "My head hath a nail in its shoe!"

These experiences, and more, all contributed in subtle and often surprising ways to my ultimate decision to dedicate my life to teaching, helping and nurturing those precious children whose disabilities sometimes obscure their rich potential for living life fully. Their stories are my story.

When I finally was able to continue my pursuit of education, I attended New York State Teachers College in Buffalo, N.Y., where I received my Masters' degree in Education in 1949. At last, my life was back on track.

New Beginnings

On February 14, 1949, I was blessed with an endowment of twenty-nine years to research and teach children with cerebral palsy. The study was conducted under the auspices of the University of Rochester School of Medicine and Dentistry. It also received assistance from New York State and through the National Foundation for Infantile Paralysis (later known as the March of Dimes).

Working with us on the program were the Day Clinic of the Cerebral Palsy Association for the Rochester Area, Inc., the Rochester Rehabilitation Center, and Public School #5 for physically handicapped children, all in Rochester, New York.

The center of this research was the Edith Hartwell Clinic (EHC), located in a beautiful mansion donated to Strong Memorial Hospital of the University of Rochester by Mrs. Ernest L. Woodward and her husband. Edith Hartwell Clinic was located atop a ribbon of driveway that left the highway heading west into nearby Leroy, New York. Funds were provided to remodel the home to be used for the study of cerebral palsy and other neuromuscular disabilities.

Thirty boys and girls received special treatment as residents. The children ranged in age up to 13 years. They were selected after examination by a committee consisting of a pediatrician, orthopedist, psychologist, neurologist and social service worker. This was a unique group for this pilot study, headed by Dr. R. Plato Schwartz, professor of orthopedic surgery of Strong Memorial Hospital in Rochester. Also on the staff were physical, occupational and speech therapists. A teacher served as a kind of educational therapist working with the medical group who advised the kind, amount and method of treatment required in the school situation for each child, a virtual prescription for treatment. I was the teacher assigned to establish the school.

Here, on that date in 1949, I stood at the entrance of the clinic, as green as beginning corn, needing help to grow and hoping for sunshine. I was twelve years older than a typical novice, frail and weak after ten years of bed care, and with no experience except fighting for my life, but with gratitude for the gift of standing at a door to be opened. My memory does not serve me today, as I write, for I don't recall my mode of arrival at this entrance, but I remember no fear of being alone! My excitement, mixed with concern for my lack of experience, and my joy at beginning my chosen work increased as the huge door opened and the head nurse greeted me with a confidence-building welcome.

I knew the grand interior of the mansion from one previous conference with the administrative staff who had interviewed me and others concerning the specifics of our positions. From the center foyer, I remember to the right, the small elegantly furnished office reception room. To the left, enclosed by ivory colored paneling, were places for wraps and supplies for visiting research personnel. Straight forward from the center foyer was the brightest room, once a huge sun parlor and now the occupational therapy area. This south wall, completely built of glass, gave a look of crystal light revealing a wooded landscape to the rear of the mansion and then a playground for children. To the right of center was an imposing pipe organ said to be a replica of the great organ at Radio City Music Hall in New York City. All elaborate furnishings were removed to make the house child-proof.

Sadly, I could see the organ was in the process of being dismantled and I still remember the ivory paneled walls torn open to pull out the pipes.

Ramps ranging approximately two steps to various doorways

rose from the sunken vestibule to work places, making the house truly accessible for handicapped children to reach all areas. Up a two-step ramp to the right and beyond the organ was the dining room with murals in green and white. Various size round tables for wheelchairs, some conventional chairs for ambulatory children and an adult aide at each table completed the furnishings. Chandeliers hung over the tables with their gorgeous branches of bulbs which had replaced the candles of earlier times. Prisms dripped from these fixtures and sparkled like diamonds in the sunlight. The kitchen adjoined the dining room.

From the center of the foyer to the left was the spacious living room paneled in teakwood from India with a fireplace spanning a third of the east wall. On the rest of this wall were windows flooding the room with sunlight and looking out on a landscape of lawn, tall Douglas pines and smaller stands of maple, oak and silver birch trees. This was to be my classroom.

All this beauty was not needed for children to develop and learn. However, the setting helped motivate the staff by providing an environment of peace and a kind of elegance not usually found in the workplace.

I remember from my initial visit that from the north of the schoolroom was an entrance to the library paneled in rich mahogany. Here staff meetings were held weekly for diagnosis and prescribed treatment for children. Here they were given individual attention with such kindness from doctors and therapists that even the very young ones had no fear.

I still remember standing with the head nurse, foyer-centered on my way to start my first class for children with cerebral palsy and other neuromuscular disabilities.

My memory is so clear because of the serenity, peace and confidence I experienced as the head nurse directed me to the schoolroom and announced that Pete had placed four multiply disabled children in wheelchairs and that they were waiting for school to start.

The French doors to the living room were open. Through the

vertical crack between the hinges, I saw eight eyes fixed on my awaited entrance. I observed a tense look of anticipation of things to come on the faces of the children. They must have promised Pete, their very special aide who loved them, to "be good and wait for the teacher" because he was busy and had to leave them.

I entered with my bag of tricks, which all teachers carry in readiness for situations in which instant visual aids are needed in emergencies.

Through another French door to the right of the great fireplace, I viewed at a glance an unforgettable sight. There was a stand of young Douglas pine trees in the yard against a deep blue sky. Every branch was lined with sparkling snow. A flock of scarlet-bright cardinals and their mates in subdued shades of orange perched on every available limb. It was a quivering picture as the birds chirped and twittered tremulously, each keeping to his own perch, as if attached to a Christmas tree. The sun created crystal gems on their meeting place. A thing of beauty!

I was troubled with indecision. How do I get the four handicapped children, whom I had not yet met, to view this spectacle? They could not stand without help. Pete was busy. Should I ring the alarm for his help the first day of school especially since he had left everything in perfect order? Was this an emergency? How long would the birds stay? Time was of the essence. "There is a way of treating all cases" was one of my principles of teaching.

"Move" I said to myself.

I greeted the children with a plan. They smiled in aphonic agreement and I immediately wheeled each chair to the window. They were seated too low in their chairs to see any part of the outdoor masterpiece. Two had athetoid cerebral palsy. None could walk or stand or balance without help.

Danny was my first endeavor. I unbuckled the belts from his ankles, waist and shoulder, slid him carefully from his chair to his feet on the floor and held him against me for his balance. Then I locked his braces. His cooperation was miraculous. My chin rested on the back of his head. He held his own weight. I could not believe an eight-year-old could be so tall.

As I described the picture in his ear, the others listened and waited patiently. Danny had no speech at all but his facial expression demonstrated interest, understanding and delight in this unusual lesson. He cooed and grunted, smiled and cooed.

There was no time to extend the joy of the moment. I pondered my next step. How could I possibly take time to fasten Danny back in his wheel-chair? It would take time. The birds would leave and the other children would have no chance to see this spectacle. I laid Danny on his back on the floor facing the blank ceiling. He couldn't fall and my responsibility for his safety was accomplished.

One down, three to go. I repeated my plan with the other three children. The birds stayed right where they were and were still happily decorating the "Christmas tree."

But now I had four small bodies lying on their backs on the floor viewing a blank ceiling and I was waiting for Pete to answer my ring for help to lift and fasten them securely in their wheelchairs.

How the children laughed! The school room looked like a disaster area but with no hard hats. The only time I recall a scenario comparable was when I visited the Sistine Chapel at the Vatican in Rome. There I saw artists lying flat on the floor and on benches studying the painting of Michelangelo's "Last Judgment."

Pete arrived amidst this scene and the children were convulsed with laughter as he lifted them one by one into their chairs. Everything accomplished with these children is time consuming. With patient gentleness, combined with Pete's physical strength, they were secured with buckles, ties, braces and brakes. Only people who love humanity and don't shun hard work should be hired to do this kind of work.... Someone like Pete with his café-au-lait complexion and strong hands on guard to help at any moment.

I learned there are countless methods of teaching. There are

21

the lecture, observation and performing methods. Then structured planning by drill and repetition to establish the neural bonds. Every way should be happy, full of enthusiasm and excitement for the learner. A teacher learns even more. She becomes the learner. The wheelchair is not a place of captivity and one should never be left alone in a chair for an extended time without something to see, to hear or to do. Without his disability, the child would run independently to the place of action. This leads to the fact that multiply-handicapped children initially might need to be "spoon fed" their education, as they are spoon fed their food. The child's teacher must know what a child's mental age is relative to his chronological age. This becomes a ratio of one to the other and actually is his intelligence quotient. How does the teacher obtain his IQ when the student cannot speak or use his hands or exhibits other disabilities?

In 1955, Elsa Hausermann, working at Columbia University Teachers College, researched and wrote extensively in this vastly difficult area of testing children with multiple neurological aberrations to ascertain mental age. Her book on adaptation of the Stanford-Binet Intelligence Test for persons with no speech and poor or no hand use is a singular contribution to research for special education. She believed that the child with cerebral palsy was "like some, like all, like no other child." Therefore he must prove in unusual ways his intelligence however hidden.

After this day of teaching, I thought of all the courses I had studied, passed and forgotten: *Psychology of the Handicapped, Methods of Teaching the Handicapped, Educational Measurements, Professional Ethics.* I wondered how they helped me become a teacher. A wise person explained to me that education is what you have left after you've forgotten what you've learned.

The two hour session with four multiply-handicapped eight year old children ended with attendant learnings too numerous to record. The birds sojourned for a long time since they were not migratory but actually lived in the area. My bag of tricks was of no use. I received no merit award for my structurally written lesson plan. I instinctively wanted the children to experience and remember the beauty in the world. Reality developed a complete and lasting lesson plan through no merit of mine. I became the learner.

God bless the shine of the sun on the snow, on the trees and on the birds on that cold February day in 1949.

Later in the day on that first afternoon, six children of pre-school level and all with cerebral palsy of varying degrees were parading across the vestibule towards the ramp leading to the schoolroom. They were assisted by Pete and three other aides. It was a sight to see and hear. Four were multiply-disabled, each with quadruple problems such as inability to speak, to walk, and poor hand use. From outward appearances they seemed of normal intelligence but their records stated that the brain injury that caused the physical handicaps could also have affected their mental abilities.

One child was hobbling independently with a cane and another held the hand of an aide. He wore what I soon would hear daily were "pillow pants". I'm still smiling about these pants and will explain later. Their histories told me that, although some could make sounds, only one had intelligible speech. Yet, they sounded like little cheerleaders and I vowed that my objective in teaching would be, "Don't break their spirit and enthusiasm for learning. Let them talk". And so I encouraged them to speak anytime provided it caused no interruption. This objective might cause me problems in the future, making for noisy situations during instruction time. However, speech had to be developed through practice.

I remember struggling patiently and endlessly with Patty, a seven year old mildly affected girl who had no intelligible speech but also no known physical impediment to speech. She seemed to pay particular attention to the story of Little Red Riding Hood.

As I reached whatever the exciting climax of the story was fifty years ago *(was it when the wolf gobbled up the grandmother?)*, I

23

must have become overly dramatic.

"And the wolf grabbed Red Riding Hood's grandmother and gobbled her up!" I said excitedly.

And that's when Patty spoke her first words, loudly and clearly. *"Son of a bitch!"*

After lunch, the six quadriplegic children in the parade would soon be seated in wooden chairs carefully designed and built by the talented EHC workmen who constructed the furniture, especially tables and chairs. The tables were adjustable, had cut-out spaces for chairs to roll in, giving support for arms during desk work. They were entirely made of wood and were designed with the back straight up to control the head. They had firm and sturdy seats and footrests to which the child's ankles could be secured, making hips and thighs form right angles to the body.

There were no large wheels on the chairs for self-propelling since the children were too young and disabled to operate them. Instead these chairs had large casters that would swivel for turns. At specific times, the child was removed from the chair and placed on a mat or table for therapy but his sitting position in the chairs at all times was right and proper.

As the children grew older, self propelling, commercially made wheelchairs were used which were less restrictive, but less posturized. They also did not fit as well into the cut out tops of the special desks with their brightly colored tops.

Now, back again to our procession of children in wooden chairs — one ambulatory, and the independent walker in "pillow pants" and all marching without banners to school! The aides helped form a semicircle of wheelchairs in the classroom and the two walkers relaxed in tiny armchairs as if waiting to be served.

I was delighted and encouraged to learn from their histories that all six of this group could hear and see. Consequently, for learning, I planned to bombard them with words by explanation, by demonstration, storytelling, and any possible method I could use to spoon-feed them the education they deserved according to their chronological and their corresponding mental ages. They would need audio-visual materials as well as many specific teaching aids for orientation in time and space.

Because of poor hand use and impaired eye-hand coordination, they needed very special methods prescribed for each child. With their hearing and sight as avenues of approach, I hoped to meet their needs for academic progress and/or simply training for everyday needs.

Because brain injury happened before, during or after birth in these cases, my plans for teaching them had to be for habilitation rather then rehabilitation. In other words, they did not need to reclaim a skill they had lost, but to learn to compensate for a skill they could not achieve. Principles and objectives in plans must always be basic in origin, however complicated or advanced the plans for instruction would become as the child progressed.

In the 1940's, I remember how completely we studied Dr. Arnold Gesell's writings on the development of the normal child from birth to five years of age. More learning -- physically, intellectually, psychologically and in all areas -- occurs during this time than in any other period of life. The congenitally brain-injured child cannot learn unless he is provided with the experiences necessary for growth in all these areas. He must be "spoon fed" his education or he will not develop physically, psychologically, and academically and will often be misperceived as retarded.

Parents are the first teachers and often the first to detect abnormalities. Then medical diagnosis and prescriptions for therapy are absolutely necessary for the child during the first five years of life. He should be exposed to all kinds of stimuli by being with people, and by being taken to places of learning, such as stores, parties, playgrounds. Even if he only observes, he will perceive and learn.

These experiences will be the basis of perception in all learning, basic and advanced.

Transportation is obviously a problem for the disabled at any age, but children can be more easily carried from place to place for learning experiences as preschoolers. Before age six, their learning ability is enhanced and the wheelchair is not a catalyst for isolation.

I was encouraged to find several of my selected group outgoing and possessed of a keen awareness as well as the ability to perceive their little worlds on a level commensurate with their chronological ages. This is a compliment to their parents.

Two bags of 'tricks" were my planned strongholds that day, one with games, puzzles, toys I kept hidden for a time. The other bag, a large brown one, was filled with every bit of nature I could gather on my way to "school." They listened with interest as I explained my living quarters in an old carriage house that was remodeled for the staff. I walked daily to class along a path through a beautiful wooded area and found tiny plants, flowers, weeds, sleeping bugs, twigs, bark, tree limbs, dried sticks, vines, nuts, stones of all sizes, dirt, bird feathers, evergreen and nests. I collected whatever I thought would interest them. The children were delighted, listening to descriptions and names of each item which they handled with one or two hands or just pushed with one knuckle around the table and onto the floor.

They became so involved there was no time for the second bag of academic tricks.

At the close of this second session, I began to feel the mountains of stress that come with the amount of work to do. I had to look ahead to find fresh approaches and new methods of instruction. There were so many possibilities that they surely outnumbered the impossibilities, and would take a whole lot longer to get through. It would take a special order of discipline, patience and love.

A disabled child is "like some, like all, like no other one." Indeed, he has a right to be taught at his chronological age level (plus or minus his mental ability) even if he responds ever so slightly to education either in a group or in tutoring.

I remember making an analogy as a young teacher when I was

reading *The Prophet* by Khalil Gibran. He wrote: "No man can reveal to you aught but that which already lies half asleep in the dawning of your knowledge!" That is not entirely true for the brilliant person with cerebral palsy whose intelligence is locked up by injury to the brain and who is not "half-asleep," but sound asleep.

Avenues of approach need to be discovered to educate each child. It just takes time and that is the one thing I had in abundance.

Pillow Pants

Something that aroused my curiosity on arrival at the Edith Hartwell Clinic was the "Fracas" splint, more commonly known as "pillow pants". This appliance was worn by infants and toddlers as a diaper except that it was about four times the thickness of extra-large, modern *Pampers*™. Infants at Hartwell wore them quite comfortably since they were carried about or lay in bed.

However, toddlers, as they came of age, fortunately became ambulatory and contending with these bulky pillows between their legs caused frequent uproars between the children and their aides. The purpose of the pillow pants in these pioneer days of study was to correct dislocated or subluxed hips by spreading the legs outward in a position to gradually replace the hips in their sockets.

All this I understood, but the word "fracas," meaning "a smash or noisy fight" did not make common sense to me. Was this how they came to be called "Fracas" splints? During the day a voice would ring out, like a cheerleader, calling for help to an aide . *"Help. B.J.'s Fracas splint has slipped!"*

Crotch-wise, the splint had to fit exactly east and west as well as north and south between the legs to be effective. Various straps were tailored up and over the shoulders from the waist, circling the waist and then attached lower to the plump little thighs to avoid slippage. All this planning, however, did not solve the problem of slipping completely.

As time passed, I found time to research this and discovered that a Dr. Freijka (pronounced Fray-ke) of Prague, Czechoslovakia, had discovered that thousands of infants in that city had dislocated or subluxed hips. His pioneer work was proven successful at the Hartwell Clinic. Today, it is called the Craig splint. But I'll never forget the "fracas" of the 1940's. The Appliance Department made and used the Freijka Splint in the 1940's for medical and diaper use.

Interestingly, in 1959, Proctor and Gamble tested its disposable diaper, *Pampers*™, in Rochester. The product appeared in 1961. I wonder now: Could the "Fracas" be the precursor of *Pampers*™?

If the Clinic had the necessary materials then for designing and making disposable diapers, such as absorbent care linings, leg cuffs, stretchy, moisture-proof plastic materials and various liners, perhaps they might have come up with something akin to *Pampers*™.

Apparently, Proctor and Gamble did not know that the Clinic had already been making and using the Freijka Splint medically and as a diaper in the 1940's. Why isn't Rochester known as the *Pampers City* instead of the Kodak City? And why aren't little guys like B.J. compensated or honored for having struggled to learn to walk with such a contraption tucked between their legs?

The Unit Activity Method

The Unit Activity Method is an integrated teaching method that enables a child to learn all of the skills he needs to know during each classroom activity. It came into use about 50 years ago. In teaching academic subjects, you teach the children to spell all the words they will use in the activity. They learn to read about all the things they will need to do as they learn to write them.

For instance, in a second grade unit they would not just learn to spell some easy word like *play* or *go* or *see*. They would learn big words like *Post Office, potato, garden,* even *agriculture.* They are being introduced to reading and spelling as a functional part of the activity. They wouldn't seriously be required to spell all of these words exactly but there would be many attendant learnings.

In math, they would learn different words appropriate to each unit such as *bushel, quart, peck.* They would learn these measurements and be introduced to the concepts. The focus need not be intense, but the learning process could encompass a whole year. For instance, a store which is operated under adult supervision, can operate indefinitely, providing an extended learning experience.

The School Store

In one corner of the teak paneled living room at the Hartwell Clinic, our older children established and operated a general store. This was a working lesson in math, social skills, organization, reading, spelling, art and socialization. It succeeded in its academic goals and it made money. This was not a script or "play-money" based economy. It was real, with prices based on what we paid when we bought the supplies plus a few cents profit. We sold things like stationery, toothpaste, postage stamps and potato chips.

The children staffed the store, made change, took orders, kept the shelves stocked, made the advertising posters, even went to town with adult staff members to shop for the merchandise. This project might be far above their actual mental ability, but we concentrated with drill on their own level. There were attendant learnings, with a great deal learned beyond the actual academics, but final objectives were based on preparing the children eventually for stricter academic instructional activities.

A schedule of times each day when the store was open was worked out. Children were scheduled to work but an adult would always be there to help the child with the actual job performance. The fine points of punching a time card and making a salary were left for the future. It was enough that the children have the satisfaction and fun of being part of a community endeavor. The store operated for the whole year or as needed to accomplish the objectives.

This Unit Activity Method, although a method devised quite long ago, was very successful, profitable and fun for both adults and children involved in education at EHC.

The Potato Patch

Another Unit Activity Method we used for teaching at Hartwell Clinic was simple gardening. We began by reading about potatoes. We selected the best spot for the garden and in the spring the custodial staff dug up a patch about 20 feet by 20 feet in a sunny area.

We had to allow for very widely spaced rows so the children could maneuver to work. The children selected potatoes with "eyes" in them, cut them in pieces and planted them. Children in wheelchairs were wheeled as far as possible and then carried to the patch. Attendants helped them dig and plant.

We also studied the "potato bug," the Colorado potato beetle and how to control it. We watered and weeded. Over the summer the custodial staff tended the garden. In the fall, we harvested a fine crop of lovely white potatoes.

With the help of the kitchen cooks, we fed the students and staff for lunch. We had mashed, French fried, baked potatoes, potato chips, potato salad and hash browns. It was a lesson in science and in home economics. The children could make the connection between the potato chips in the bag from the store and the small white round vegetable they picked out of the ground several months after they planted the seed.

It was also a lesson for adult staff and showed how cooperation and dedication on the part of the whole school community can make learning successful, valuable, and rewarding. If it is fun for the adults, it is also fun for the children who will learn.

However, this project was not a simple endeavor, physically speaking, for aides or children. It was laborious. Sometimes two adults were needed to maneuver each wheelchair and to lift children from chair to the good earth.

However, the satisfaction gained was unforgettable.

Conversation Board

Long before augmentive communication devices were available, I began work on a low-tech (by today's standards) communication board in 1949. A second grader of mine who had multiple handicaps and was in a wheelchair gave me the opportunity to make a simple, handmade board. Dickie had a toy wind-up car that was sitting on the horizontal footrest of his Hartwell wheelchair. Having no speech and only minimal use of his fisted hand, he kept trying to get the attention of the adults and pointing to the toy car. Adults would say, "Oh yes, Dickie, what a nice car," and then walk away.

One day, the speech therapist was engaging him in a lesson when she pointed through the window to the beautiful blue sky and to the young blossoms and leaves on the tree. "Look, Dickie, what a lovely spring day."

He pounced on the word *spring* and then pointed to his car. He knew the word, but could not say it although he realized its meaning. (Think of Helen Keller discovering the word *water*!)

Sure enough, when the therapist investigated, the spring on his mechanical car had broken and needed to be replaced.

That "epiphany" led me to try and find a way for these children to communicate that was language-based, visual, graphic and economically within the reach of parents of modest means. I began to work on a small, sturdy laptop board that children could point to even if they could only point with a knuckle, like Dickie.

I began with the uppercase alphabet and numbers 1 to 0, spaced so that a child with problems of fine motor coordination could point to each letter comfortably. This took up the lower part of the board.

Across the top were commonly used words in basic English, including question words that all children used, such as *why, when, how*. The placement of these elements was standardized so that as the child progressed and we added more words, the same words would always be in the same place. I began tailoring the communication board for the children who required it.

In 1952, when I moved to the #5 School in Rochester the conversation board and the idea came along with me.

As is true with so many developments in all areas of human endeavor, I was not the only person working on the idea of enhancing the communication of people with handicaps.

Our speech therapist at the Clinic had told me of a young gentleman with cerebral palsy named F. Hall Roe of Chicago who had developed his own communication board. An inquiry to the Mercy Free Dispensary in Chicago got me in touch with Mr. Roe and a warm and friendly correspondence developed.

He explained that while in high school, he had developed his own small spelling chart, hand written on the back cover of a notebook, to assist his teachers in understanding his rather limited speech. This grew into more advanced and sophisticated versions as he went on to college and into the workplace.

He was most generous in sharing his ideas and encouraging my work. In addition to letters, he sent me a copy of a speech he had given in 1948 to the Parents' Association for Spastic Children's Aid in Chicago as well as a tracing of his current board. During our correspondence, he moved to St. Paul, Minnesota to work as a writer in the public relations department of St. John's Hospital.

While at #5 School, I compiled an in-service study guide entitled "Aphonic Communication for Those with Cerebral Palsy" which was published in 1960 by the New York State Cerebral Palsy Association.

Onward and Upward to Rochester

AFTER THREE YEARS' RESEARCH in cerebral palsy at the Edith Hartwell Clinic under the auspices of the University of Rochester School of Medicine and Dentistry, I seriously considered working with children with various handicaps and especially those with average or above intelligence in the public elementary schools.

But in 1951, before even applying, I was offered a position in the Rochester City School District at John Williams School #5 in the Orthopedic Department. I was interviewed by Dr. Herman Goldberg, then Director of Special Education and soon to become Superintendent of Rochester City Public Schools. Also present was Miss Ethel Pease, principal of #5 school. Both were well known educators who had been frequent visitors observing the research at Edith Hartwell over the preceding two years.

I had no written resume of qualifications for any kind of teaching position. Perhaps resumes were not in style 50 years ago, but an oral interview sufficed since my interviewers were aware of my degree from Buffalo State University and had also observed my work at the Clinic. This gave me a step up in securing the position.

I remember clearly my interviewers' two direct questions. First, "What are your principles for teaching handicapped children?"

My response was that there is basically no difference between teaching so-called 'normal' and handicapped children. I added that their imperative needs are the same and that there must be an order of discipline in learning. There must be love all around for people. There must be generosity on the part of the teacher in exposing every child to all knowledge at his age level regardless of his physical ability.

If a child's physical ability is so dysfunctional that he cannot perform to learn, then he must be "spoon fed" the knowledge appropriate to his mental age. In addition, there must be readiness in the child's physical and mental development and a willingness on the part of the teacher to work to recognize every need.

Starting with very basic experiences initially, the teacher's approach must move from the concrete to the abstract as the child advances or regresses. The child's readiness to progress at each stage takes careful observation to ascertain.

The second question they posed still makes me laugh and leaves me rather shamefaced since my honest answers were so simplistic. "What do you do when disciplining handicapped, very young children in pain if extremely stressful situations arise?"

I replied, "I groan audibly and dramatically to get their attention and say 'I'm going to turn into a bear and I'm going to growl!' (Children are such believers!)

"Laughter usually follows and the work goes on."

I continued, "When tension peaks in an older group of little ones, I stop all activity and announce, 'You are more trouble to me than all my money!' I taught them to raise their hands at this announcement and in cheerleader fashion, with hands held high, to shout 'What money?' Laughter follows and stress lessens." (This may sound rather corny today but it was very effective 50 years ago).

I remember wondering what to try for discipline in the case of a 4th or 5th grader and recall saying, "How could a good boy do a thing like this?" Above all, there must be love and then all problems that need reprimand can often be corrected.

My interviewers left and I climbed two flights of stairs to the third floor. Yes, the Orthopedic Department of School #5 with its wheelchairs, braces, canes, crutches, plinths, therapy and school rooms and all the beautiful little people with problems of muscles, bones and joints were "four flights down from Seventh Heaven".

I loved every inch of its height.

The Building Plant

Years prior to my coming in 1952, the founders of the Orthopedic Department had no alternative but to accept the offer of a third floor in such a substantially built school. I was later to learn that in the 1920's, during a terrible outbreak of poliomyelitis, the third floor of #5 School was used to care for polio patients. Then, with the development of a vaccine to prevent polio by Dr. Jonas E. Salk, a U.S. bacteriologist, the third floor soon became available as a place for orthopedically handicapped children until 1965.

Despite its location on the third floor, it actually had some excellent features. There were six spacious classrooms, a music room, a large dining area furnished with attractive large, medium and small oval wooden tables painted teal blue, with chairs to match, just the correct size for each child whether in a wheelchair or ambulatory.

The large windows facing North Plymouth Avenue almost reached the ceiling, giving light, sunshine and clean air. Standing in the corner of each room was a long pole with end hooks which was used to open and close the high windows.

The wide corridors made it possible for children in wheelchairs to travel according to traffic rules, as if on a major highway, watching for pedestrians and vehicles entering from side streets (rooms).

The classrooms also were spacious, which proved that the founders were cognizant of the fact that handicapped non-ambulatory children needed space, for instance, to park their chairs then slide into available so-called normal chairs for school activities. There was also space for canes, braces and crutches that had to be placed carefully to prevent walkers from tripping over them but still conveniently located for the owner's immediate use. Many children wore the Craig splint, which needed a full 180° of space for the wearer to simply stand, turn, and then walk.

I must not forget the old freight elevator which had to be large enough to lift children daily to the third floor. There were all sizes of chairs from man-size for big boys and girls to tiny doll size. I never had time to estimate the number of trips daily but the old "el" traveled constantly, operated by the janitor who never considered it a chore.

There was love all around. One could truly believe the saying that "There is no man so straight as one who would bend to help a child." This was the character of our janitor.

Fire Drills

The most serious duty of staff in any building having disabled people is to have ready a safe, sound plan for fire escapes. Stairways and elevators are forbidden for exit and are not always accessible in an emergency. A plan by the administration had been perfected long before my days at #5 School began in 1952. I am still impressed by the speed and safety of the procedure. It proves that the impossible becomes possible with patience and time and an educated plan.

Although the siren announcing each drill was startling, there seemed to be no fear; just a need to move. The children would be scattered throughout the department, in therapy, restrooms, in corridors, music room, physical education or classrooms.

Every adult had an assignment. Extra wooden folding chairs on wheels were available in all the classrooms for ambulatory children who were slow walkers. Those who could walk were taken by the hand by an adult.

Within a minute or two after the sound of the alarm, the regular 6th graders from the 2nd floor arrived at their appointed stations on the 3rd floor. Two strong, alert, 'life-savers' were needed for each wheelchair, one to push the chair and the other to act as a brake.

They would wheel each chair carefully across a large area of outdoor roof space, which was the ceiling of the lower floor over the gymnasium. Then they had to maneuver the chairs down a two story chute. This sounds like a frightening ordeal, but I must explain, it was not a sharp drop, but rather like a long, steep, modified ramp.

Both the pusher and the braker, who had to walk backwards as he held on to the front of the wheelchair, had to pay strict attention. There were hairpin turns with adults stationed at each turn to stop a possible runaway chair.

The ambulatory children walked holding the hand of a guide or 6th grader. Any sign of excitement and joy expressed by the children

36

had to be discouraged for the sake of safety even if it seemed to some of them like a great adventure.

The landing in the parking area in the rear of the school was the climax to this highly supervised roller coaster ride. We chuckled over the tiny walker who said "Our feet slipped down to the toes of our shoes going down the ramp!"

At the "All safe"signal, our trip back to the third floor via the old reliable elevator was a familiar and relaxing ride.

As I reflect back on that experience, I feel that the 6th grade boys and girls who acted as pushers and brakers of wheelchairs along that steep passageway to safety with their handicapped peers must have experienced satisfaction and an education beyond the classroom. I wonder also if the same appreciation and gratitude stayed with them when the Orthopedic Department moved to the first floor of the Adlai E. Stevenson School #29 on Kirkland Avenue in 1965.

Public School Staff

I recall that I was blessed with excellent principals during my teaching years. One school of a thousand pupils would have a principal, an assistant principal, as well as supervisors to oversee various areas of the curriculum. These supervisors came from the Central Office of the Rochester City School District at appointed times.

I barely remember being observed by these special supervisors, but I do recall how exacting and difficult it was to obtain a position for special education teaching in the 1950's. Supervisors from the Central Office would travel to as many as forty schools in the city to assist beginning teachers.

In orthopedic classes, there was daily communication with therapists and parents. If a child were absent at arrival time with no written message from the bus driver, a telephone call was made to the home. However, supervision by other academic supervisors in the regular departments, where children were more independent, was more limited. Today, I admit to being surprised that so many principals and supervisors are needed to operate a school system.

Certainly, the rise of technology, the increase in crime, the problem of discipline and the many choices available in public education make for extreme changes in attendance. While I am reluctant to criticize, it does seem to be caused by an extreme lack of discipline by parents and teachers. Teachers should be talented, resourceful, willing to make hard decisions, enforce rules, be generous with both information and kindness, and be supported financially and in discipline matters. Success in teaching derives from the resourcefulness of the teacher who can spread enthusiasm and interest for attendance. Too many students today do not come to school to learn.

I recall enjoying distinguished and competent principals in my years of teaching. They dealt with daily dilemmas and problems arising in the inner city streets surrounding their neighborhood schools. These problems came daily to the school office and had to be resolved. Even so, peace reigned to a greater degree than today.

One principal played his violin during lunch hour with accompaniment by a teacher. This was possible because most pupils went home for lunch since it was a neighborhood school. His time out for music seemed appropriate and fitting.

Another principal was exceedingly talented in organizing both curricular and extra-curricular activities despite many conflicts in plans, classes, special subjects, therapies and sports.

One of my favorite principals was a major in psychology. Chronologically, she was a young senior citizen, talented, out-spoken, impartial, unbiased and an avid reader who regaled us often with her humor. She was a master of dealing with people, insisting that her teachers speak out especially when disagreements arose and always at teacher meetings.

I especially remember her tangle with the old freight elevator. Her office was on the first floor and it was required that each teacher have a "license" to operate the elevator. Being less than mechanically inclined, she needed six months to learn and pass the test. On the day she received her "certification," she marched, without banners, down the corridor and clearly vocalized, adapting a popular advertising slogan of the day, *"Today I operated the freight elevator of John Williams School #5 in my new Maiden Form bra!"*

I remember the half-days when the children were dismissed before lunch so that teachers and administrators could hold conferences on the curriculum. There was much discussion and discourse, pros and cons, on subjects such as methods of teaching or selection of new textbooks. It was time usually well spent, but often policies and procedures of the school were covertly determined by a committee prior to the meeting.

I listened, contributed, learned to understand various methods, and used them all as a beginner but finally realized some of the various methods should be used subject to the teacher's discretion. When we tried the Cluster Method, one parent telephoned and said, *"I don't want my Harry cloistered!"*

The Unit Activity Method and the Individualization Method were all effective in certain situations, and perhaps they are needed but I feel the teacher must select the most appropriate way to teach.

Teaching is an art and "no written word nor spoken plea can teach young hearts what men should be. Not all the books on all the shelves, but what the teachers are themselves."

No legislation by state or federal government can solve the daily problems teachers face, nor can all the computers in Silicon Valley. I remember returning to my classroom after conferences, closing the door, and doing it my way!

The comic strip *Peanuts* by Charles Schultz was created in 1950, just in time to help me with necessary common sense. I loved Charlie Brown with his oversized, macrocephalic head. How filled with practical ideas and how very generous with his quick answers. He relieved unknown mountains of tension and stress and preached with economy of words that personal happiness came from within. He was sharp and blunt.

Each year in March during my 29 years of teaching, I reserved a 6 x 4 ft bulletin board in my classroom for *Peanuts*. On it was a large colorful cut-out of Charlie Brown firmly holding the string of a kite blowing in the breeze created by a radiator below. Snoopy was the audience. The caption clearly said "GO FLY A KITE!"

My apologies to the Administration. I'm sure orders were sent from the Central Office for administrators to hold regular teacher conferences, and to fill their agenda with goodies.

They still do it today just as they did 50 years ago.

Mainstreaming vs. Classification

I remember that in many, moderate-sized cities there might be a total of 75 or more children of various chronological ages with physical disabilities, needing special placement in school. This was my situation in Rochester.

It provided for actual classification for grades one through six. It allowed for ideal socialization at various age levels with a complete department of physical, occupational and speech therapies delivering treatment in one place.

Children with mental retardation were in special classes but disabled children with average or above average intelligence received an academic curriculum for skills preparing them for transfer to the elementary departments of their own district schools.

This is what was called *mainstreaming* in the 1960's, but it was not always a quick, easy and accurate process. It was believed by pioneers in the field, that no child should be transferred from the Orthopedic Department until he had already developed the ability and skills to cope in a regular class.

The changes that followed in the 1970's (what is now called *mainstreaming*) were driven by economic and financial problems and often happened at children's expense. Parents were excited about this change thinking it was a sign of progress for their children. In some cases it was progress; but in others, it was a disaster.

The Home School program (learning at home) would have been far superior from the primary through 4th grade, provided the child did not need therapy. However, in most cases, the child would miss the important factor of socialization with peers. For him to benefit, he needed the social, medical and educational facilities available in the Orthopedic Department of a larger public school.

Change or choice is not always progress. Long hours of bus travel from outlying areas causes exhaustion at the beginning of the school day. There are pros and cons *ad infinitum* to treating and educating children with disabilities.

This doesn't mean that all disabled children need to live in a large public school district. A disabled child alone in a small-sized school district can learn and grow provided all his most imperative needs for independent life are fulfilled. His parents must understand and appreciate his medical needs, and his teachers need to know and practice correct educational procedures.

My experience in Rochester was excellent because we had the essentials of a wonderful staff and good Central Office direction, even when I was beginning in 1950 at a time when several teachers and therapists were retiring.

The new staff could enjoy the findings and research, and the love, interest and humor the pioneers left for them and the children. One physical therapist entertained us by telling of coming to Rochester in a "covered wagon."

She regaled all with her rich fund of stories, many of which were based on actual experiences.

Staff Medical Meetings

Staff medical meetings were held bi-monthly or privately in emergencies, both in the public school situation and at Edith Hartwell Clinic. Timely reports were received and new prescriptions dictated by the doctors to therapists and the teacher.

All staff members knew what orders were marked for a child's treatment even though an individual staff member was responsible to carry out the order. The nurse administers medication; the therapists have their work and follow prescriptions; the teacher sees that a child is standing up to two hours with braces locked, in the classroom, or sitting a length of time or walking as prescribed.

I found it interesting to affirm my belief that everyone in a position to treat children is a teacher. A neurologist examining a 12 year old boy, mistakenly used the word "disease."

This caused a cry of distress from the boy. The doctor immediately recovered saying "Jack, do you study prefixes? Do you know the word 'ease.' Are you at ease now?"

Jack answered, "Yes."

The doctor continued, "Are you upset now?"

Jack said, "No."

The doctor explained, "You see, you can be at ease or at dis-ease." The child understood and all was calm.

Another doctor the children enjoyed was called Johnny Johnston. Speaking to my third graders, he told them that his six month old baby girl was going to marry a very rich man and that she had told him that very morning who it was. Of course they asked for an explanation and he replied, "Well, she was laying in bed making baby noises when I asked who she planned to marry, and I clearly heard her say, 'Aga Khan! Aga Khan!'"

I insisted that he explain as soon as possible and left him with the children for several minutes.

Everyone dealing with children should teach.

My experience in teaching multiply-disabled children in Rochester from 1949 to 1978 spanned grades K-6 in John Williamson School #5, and later in Adlai E. Stevenson School #29. All available treatments in physical, occupational and speech therapies were provided in addition to physical education, music and art classes.

There was no confusion 50 years ago. When a child developed proper skills for readiness in his home school district, he was transferred to that district. However, competition was too strenuous in many cases compared to #5 School. (After all, there were five large classrooms on the third floor of #5 School, each consisting of 2 to 3 levels of academic ability and 12 or more children were enrolled in each, receiving individual instruction as needed. Not so back in the home district.)

Yearly enrollment in the department averaged about 75. The largest group, by disability, were children with cerebral palsy (seven types). Next were those with spina bifida, muscular dystrophy, various spinal cord problems, juvenile arthritis, sickle cell anemia and -- fortunately fading away in 1952 -- poliomyelitis.

Working with the Primary Grades

I REMEMBER TEACHING DISABLED CHILDREN as if it all happened yesterday, as unforgettable events crowd my mind with the memory of children's faces real, dear, and sweet. And the nicest thing about it is that I have not had to write one word of fiction to tell my story.

The first level I taught were grades one and two combined, and all of the children had severe disabilities. The size of the class could vary from 6 to 10 children according to the severity and number of various handicaps.

In an average year the orthopedic roster of #5 School listed 70 disabled children. The largest group were some 40 children with cerebral palsy. Then there were 12 with spina bifida, 3 with muscular dystrophy and the rest had various conditions such as spinal cord injury and sickle cell anemia. Several children were amputees.

I found the multiple grade grouping (1-2) excellent for learning since children learn from each other while the teacher exposes them to new experiences and guides the learning process for each child.

A child with an orthopedic disability may be a year or more older than his tested (IQ) grade level. This is not because of mental deficiency or mental retardation but because children with congenital injury are deprived of normal physical development from birth, and are socially isolated from their peers during the most critical years, birth to 6 years. This most precious time for growth is delayed and often not recovered, creating gaps in their academic progress.

Some children with cerebral palsy are constantly with adults from birth, unless they are fortunate enough to have siblings. For instance, Bobby and Jimmy, both with cerebral palsy, were the same age and with the same orthopedic diagnosis. Both had had the same surgery, but Bobby could walk and Jimmy could not.

They were talking about why they were different and Bobby, in an attempt at compassion, told Jimmy "but I was destined to walk." These boys were second graders.

Beginning school is an awakening. The little ones are unaware of their physical difference from others. This leaves them wide awake and ready to learn. They need to have their curiosity satisfied. They need to develop intellectual independence, social efficiency and practical life activities suited to their state in life. They need various methods of teaching to learn to read. All these objectives and skills necessitate the bedrock basic kind of teaching for building concepts so that abstract future learnings can be achieved.

The disabled child is "like some, like all, like no other one." They need the best of everything, yet each presents a unique opportunity and a unique challenge. Terms like "under-privileged" or "marginal" should not be applied to them.

None of the above can be accomplished by the teacher without the help of experienced aides who care for the children's personal needs while they are learning. Our department was fortunate to be assisted by women from the Rochester Junior Guild for Crippled Children, Inc., who helped with academic work in the classroom and assisted with field trips. The attention, comfort, joy and success these women brought to the children were cherished and priceless gifts.

I cannot remember using a written plan to teach, since specific learnings were taught individually. The desire and the ability to read is more or less innate in most children. In fact, many learned to read in a short time, often with little instruction. However, mathematics and penmanship had to be acquired by teaching and drill that we tried to make interesting and fun. Because reading opens so many doors and windows for a child, it received first priority.

Reading also had to be correlated with other daily activities.

With poor hand dexterity, especially with cerebral palsy, the teacher or aide is constantly "serving" the student. It was necessary to build oral vocabulary and word concepts, regardless of speech capability. Since these abilities were often not present or were too difficult to contend with, I used colorful and interesting books, games, toys, illustrations and visual aids for motivation.

I read the classics to them on their own level for enrichment to increase vocabulary. I remember that most disabled first graders were readers on entering school.

I remember reading "Heidi" to the children one day when Judy completely erased my written plan for the day's lesson. I began to read ". . . and Heidi went to the mountains to stay with her grandfather and his goats."

Judy, who had spina bifida, asked immediately, "Do goats have grandfathers?"

I always encouraged the children to ask questions as we went along to be sure that they were following the sense of the story. So I answered, "Yes, Judy, goats do have grandfathers."

The lesson then turned to a discussion and an explanation of the differences between animals and humans and how animals often get separated from their parents and grandparents and don't even know them, but that people are different. Then I taught the "big" word *genealogy* and made statements for their questions. The written lesson plan was transferred to the next day.

Attendant learnings pop up everywhere while young children are playing and acting and a definite plan cannot be laid out in anticipation of a child's thoughts. Words are important and children need to be bombarded with them.

I subscribed to a primary grade newspaper with many captioned pictures. We called this weekly newspaper a kind of *literature*. In a particular issue it told that one family in two keeps some kind of pet. Of these pets, about 26 million were dogs and more than a million and a half of these were poodles or beagles.

That led to a discussion about large animals, extra-large ones and small ones. These were all the attendant learnings. For instance, an elephant would not make a good pet. Of course, the word *litter* was discussed. I asked "Why do you think there were so many home pets that were poodles or beagles?" Jamie, who had arthritis, offered "It must be because of the large *litter-ature.*"

I had no doubt the pun was intended.

This led to more explanations about the difference between *litter* and *literature*. As I said, attendant learnings pop up everywhere.

I recall another incident as we "read" pictures and the story said a mouse "gnawed." Phonetically, I demonstrated on the chalkboard that the letter *g* was silent in this word. Jamie offered the meaning "You know, like you say 'Naw, I don't want to go'."

In his own way, he was learning that some words sound alike but have entirely different meanings. And not all are homonyms.

A large, comprehensible oral vocabulary is a necessary prerequisite for reading at the primary level. I never wrestled with the ABCs in a structural, formal method but with colorful books, stories, films and activities for exposure to learn shapes, colors and sounds in language to broaden their concentration.

I wanted to tickle them with a love of learning.

As a beginning teacher, I made mistakes. Fifty years ago there was a trend toward emphasizing word recognition. For instance, John's sentence read "The boy rode straight down the road on his bicycle." John know all the words except *straight*. I remember acting out, with every possible charade, physical clues for this word. His best guess was "the boy went *lickety split.*"

Then there was another instance of multiple choice – "the calf fell in a little hole and was_____ (tame, came, lame, game)." John's answer was "dead."

His reasoning deserved an A+ and my grade should have been zero. If it continued, I could have spent my life's teaching career in a clown suit! We need to remember that teaching is an art with designs and methods subject to change. The most effective way is a prescription of phonics and other methods served up as needed.

It was often a puzzle to ascertain what a child found important to announce. I remember Bill saying "I have a "th" in my pocket."

On emptying his pocket, I discovered he was returning his phonics homework.

Arithmetic activities for readiness were often more stressful than reading requisites, perhaps because number knowledge is not as innate. Primary grade children also need to explore relationships in numbers by manipulating concrete materials in order to acquire learning concepts for abstract reasoning. Without good hand use, problem solving and computational skills are difficult to acquire.

The child with multiple disabilities must be provided with number games, films and activities of everyday life, and our teachers' aides were a big help in using these with the handicapped. Bedrock basics were an important part of our math instruction in the primary sections to prepare the children for third grade symbolization.

As long as classes were small enough, it was possible to cover all of the educational basics in teaching the very young with the assistance of teacher's aides' loving hands.

Children with disabilities move slowly while teacher and aides must move rapidly and constantly to keep the children mentally alert and motivated. Standing and bending over tiny desks was hazardous for any teacher. For a time, I wore a long necklace which the children loved. This caught in their hair as I bent over a desk to help them — causing much laughter and fun as the necklace tangled with a child's hair which had to be cut away in gobs simply to release me.

Some improvement occurred when I borrowed a therapist's stool with large casters, allowing me to sit and ride the aisles. This idea was excellent and served me for years. "Like some, like all," my ambulatory children were fascinated by the wheels. Consequently, strict rules for safety forbade playing with the stool in the classroom.

Teaching disabled children to write was psychologically difficult because poor hand use or lack of coordination made it impossible for some to hold a pencil or crayon and the child could easily become discouraged. While we had appliances for hands, nothing was effective or practical. Some handwriting was beautiful; some met their potential; some used electric typewriters. In still others, the teacher and aides simple "loaned" their hands to give the children a degree of encouragement and empowerment.

Speaking of appliances or other mechanical devices suggested for children with poor hand coordination, as in cerebral palsy, I remember refusing to cooperate. However, I agreed to try a page turning device. Every page of the book was laced with string, and each string led to a center point with a battery and a button to press with one finger. Pressing the button triggered a system to turn a page.

Then I saw Dick, who had cerebral palsy, with his one finger making sudden, spasmodic starts and stops, fanning himself as the pages whizzed by. It was a hot day and Dick was delighted. He had discovered a use for the device the inventor never intended. I allowed him the pleasure but the printed word for reading was never involved. The device was taken away the next day.

I have boasted that I never experienced a disciplinary problem in 29 years. If this is difficult for the reader to believe, perhaps it is because my definition of discipline is different. My idea of discipline is *order in learning*. When a child created disorder during a lesson, he was asked politely to leave the group to rest in a chair facing the door of the classroom (not the corner). Should a visitor appear in the doorway, the child being reprimanded could walk or wheel away. He understood that he was being punished by his school group and was not being humiliated in front of outsiders. He was there to sit, look, listen and learn. It worked. This was my early version of Time Out.

One could write volumes on the very first learning of primary level children with disabilities because of their multiple needs in language, sensorial, social and cultural areas, and even more in their basic academic needs.

One of my unforgettable memories is the way the capable little ones would walk about helping other children to hold their hands on their hearts for the Pledge of Allegiance.

Watching them was so moving that these children could easily have traveled the whole USA raising funds for health and education every year and would have set records for success.

Portrait of a Teacher

These snapshots in time illustrate the making of a dedicated teacher
from her earliest childhood memories through the difficult challenges of growing up in the 1920's and '30's to a career marked by
dedication, ingenuity and service to others. At first, her vocation to
teaching seemed serendipitous and unplanned, but as she responded
to the opportunities that came her way, it gradually unfolded and
flowered into a beautiful testament to the power of what one person
can do. Encouraged by mentors and sustained by lifelong friends
like Winifred Fletcher who shared her passion for educating children with disabilities, Anne Remis spent the next 29 years bringing
a revolution of hope to children with disabilities.

*Anne Remis, left, with her friend Winifred Fletcher, with whom she shared a
lifelong commitment to the education of children with disabilities.*

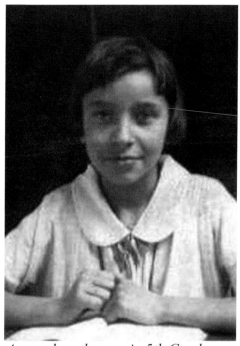

Anne when she was in 5th Grade.

Anne with her sister Dorothy in 1926

Traditional pose taken after Anne received her First Communion in 1921

Next page:
Dorothy's First Communion was the occasion for this family portrait in 1920. From the left are Anne, her mother Anna, oldest brother John, younger brother Stephen, older brother Fran, her father Frank, and sister Dorothy, more familiarly known as Dory. At the time, Anna was expecting a newcomer to the family, Anne's youngest brother George.

Dorothy (Dory) and Anne enjoy a swim in Oriskany Creek with their cousins, Molly, Alfie and Rosemary Brady from N.J. in the late 1920's.

Anne served as maid of honor at George and Grace Remis' wedding in 1949. George's friend and next-door neighbor, John Falbo, served as best man.

1935: Anne received her B.S. in Education from Oswego State Normal School

Anne spent nearly a decade recovering from tuberculosis at the famed Trudeau Sanatorium in upstate N.Y.

By 1946, her recovery progressing well, Anne could enjoy the outdoors again during family visits.

By 1949 Anne had earned her Masters Degree in education at N.Y. State Teachers in Buffalo.

Anne began her long teaching career at Edith Hartwell Clinic in Leroy, N.Y., in February, 1949.

Preceding page: Anne supervises during an ungraded class at Public School #29 in the early '70's. Andrea Levy, a favorite student, is third from the right.

Above: Anne's classroom was occasionally visited by local school officials eager to observe her innovative methods for teaching children with disabilities.

1951: *Children in Anne's class at Edith Hartwell Clinic actively celebrated*
Washington and Lincoln's birthdays by making their own hand puppets.

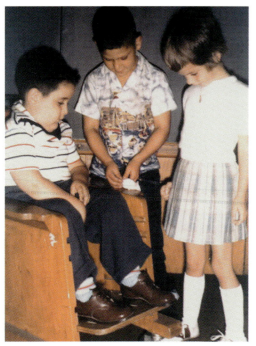

Photo taken shortly after
Anne retired from her
teaching career.

Classmates play with a pet mouse.
One is seated in a "Hartwell chair."

Two of Anne's special students were Ann Kurz, right, and Andrea Levy, shown below with her brother Marc. Ann and Andrea became lifelong friends while attending Anne's class at Public School #29 in Rochester, and both went on to lives of considerable achievement. Ann graduated from Trinity College in Washington, and received a Master's degree in computer science from the University of Rochester and is now active in her church and her community. Andrea graduated from St. John Fisher College and then went on to receive her Master's degree in Social Work at Syracuse University. See text for their full story.

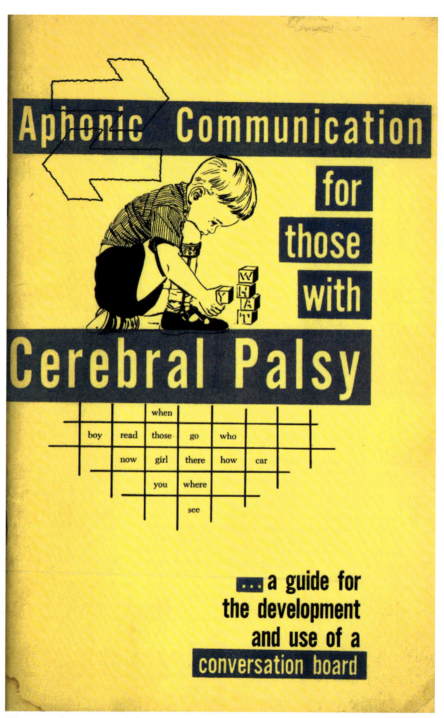

This guide to use of the conversation board was developed as a result of Anne's work and that of F. Roe Hall. He and Anne shared ideas through a 10-year correspondence in the 1950's.

Here a student uses an early version of the conversation board at Edith Hartwell Clinic with assistance from a young aide. These early developments in aphonic communication paved the way for today's more advanced devices.

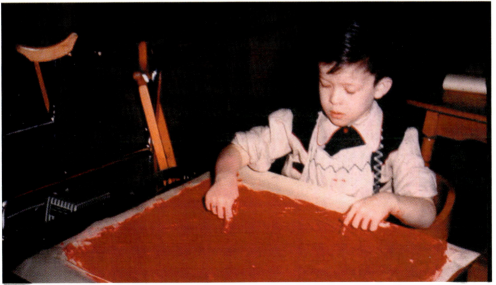

Tactile experiences like finger painting are important ways of teaching and motivating students with poor hand coordination or who lack speech.

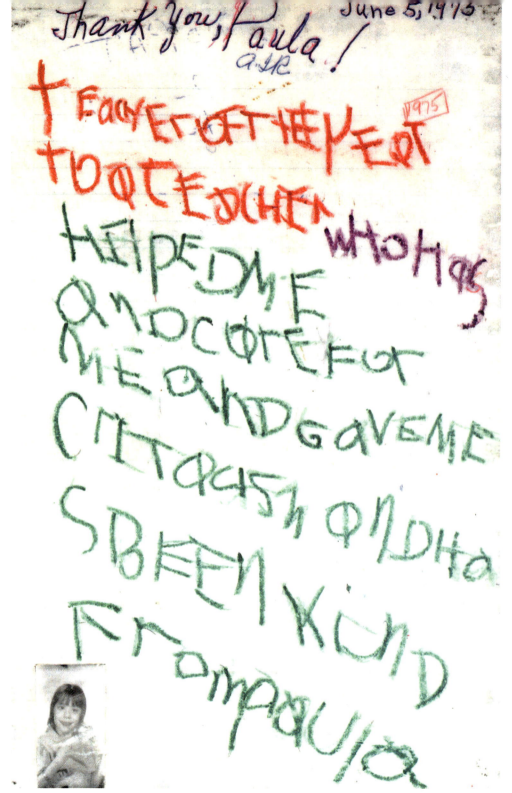

A note from a student named Paula reads: "To a teacher who has helped me and cared for me and gave me critacism (sic) and who has been kind" reflects the affection which many students felt for their favorite teacher, Anne Remis.

Moving on to New Challenges

I FELT A BIT SAD when I was assigned to teach the next higher level in the Orthopedic Department at #5 School. No situation could be more satisfying and delightful than working with the little ones who were positively full of life. There was daily fun, laughter, and a wide-eyed demand to learn. They needed no external motivation for any kind of subject matter. Working with them you learned how to salute the flag of your country with all your heart even if you could not use your hands. Volumes could be written describing how to teach children with handicaps. One sentence would sum it all up. "Use common sense and respond to their needs from your heart."

The primary children were unique, individual, self-absorbed, spontaneously working and playing along, and yet barely able to communicate with each other in speech. I dreaded losing them, but soon was at home with this next level.

I'll never forget my first day with third to fourth grade children. They were each "like some, like all, like no other one." They were curious, noisy, anxious for activity and communicated with each other in speech, however difficult for them. They experimented with all the devices in the classroom, cluttered the room with a trail of games, play and books. Progress in all areas shone clearly, except for one negative factor in their makeup. At this age, they were becoming aware of their disabilities, causing added stress for themselves. It was also stressful for me in determining methods and objectives in my daily plans to guide them psychologically.

That first day I allowed a short period of free play to observe their personalities and needs. One tiny 3rd grader, ambulatory and with no visible disability, walked about with his hands clasped behind him, to capture my attention.

He asked, "How do you say I love you in Spanish?"

"Yo te quiero," I said.

He walked away, only to return with another question, "How do you say I love you a lot?" "Yo te quiero mucho," I answered. He promptly said ,"Yo te quero mucho to you!"

He walked away with hands clasped behind him, my gift, to him, to show he was both needed and wanted.

This third grade level would be a challenge to me, but the fourth grade level still had stars in their eyes along with a look of maturity. We would work and learn together.

Academic Plans

School requires that children learn to read, write and explore numbers. This structured, academic education can be wrestled with in less than 2 hours a day, leaving much time for continuous learnings of significance, consequence and value. Academic and attendant knowledge continues apace as children progress through the elementary grades.

I found success with a chalk board-lecture method combining talk with writing and art work, including the use of diagrams, pictures and letters. The children's attention span was excellent.

Through experience I found there are many methods for teaching children with handicaps. Being disabled, they were happy to sit, listen and look, with relief from stress and pain from movement. You have to go with the method that is most expedient. I recommend that student teachers should minor in art, thereby enhancing their skills for this kind of lecture method.

Reading skills were always a priority. Details such as writing and turning pages for each child need the help of aides who are always happy to volunteer. It is difficult for the child with cerebral palsy to read in many cases. Besides poor hand use to turn pages, problems with eye focus are impediments.

When teaching individually, I sat opposite the child. His book would be on a bookstand facing him. I found it necessary to trace out his way across the page from left to right, with a pointer. Being seated opposite him, I learned to read upside down. I could see if the child's focus was a problem and also if his eyes did not move smoothly from left to right.

We had a remarkable ophthalmology consultant, Dr. Hobart Lerner, who gave his time and expertise to care for children with cerebral palsy in Rochester. These children have the same problems as other children but more frequently and under conditions that make treatment more difficult. Dr. Lerner had a way of making the complicated clear to all.

In teaching reading to children with cerebral palsy, I also detected that books were not designed properly for them. Lines were often too long for their eyes to move smoothly from left to right.

I therefore rewrote stories on more narrow pages. This made sense when I considered that when I listed my groceries in a column, my eyes moved up and down with more speed and accuracy. Can you imagine reading a grocery list written as one long paragraph?

There are always new ways for learning but there are no substitutes for interesting, colorful books that stay open, or for bulletin board displays, artwork, and films that encourage children to use the library.

Another new approach I used in reading was to have the aide or teacher act as the narrator and the child as the speaker much like reading a play where a number of children can take part. This method speeds the process and those with no oral speech can take part in whatever way they can. Sometimes this may only be a nod, a smile or a grunt.

Literature

I read the classics at each grade level because there could be no chronological gaps in their learning if their mental age was to keep pace with their chronological age.

I remember reading *Aesop's Fables,* which contain a lesson in each story, for a fourth grade class. The lesson in this story asked why you should not "count your chickens before they hatch". I had various answers but Alfie, a boy with muscular dystrophy, gave the answer that made the most sense. "You should not count your chickens before they hatch because some of them might be roosters."

Grammar and spelling start at approximately grade 3.

Often it is difficult for the teacher to teach a skill that is detailed, complicated or abstract to a multiply-handicapped child, but it is necessary to do so.

During one third grade lesson the children were taking turns at the chalkboard. The assignment was to write a complete sentence.

Joey, using his right hand only and sitting sideways in a wheelchair, worked away patiently. When finished he asked me, "How do you like it?"

I told him it was a perfect sentence. It had a capital letter at the beginning and a period at the end. It had a subject and a predicate and correct spelling.

"But" I asked Joey, "why didn't you choose a better topic?"

He said, "Because I wanted to be perfect and these are the only words I really know how to spell."

He had written, "Miss Teach is a dog!"

Spelling is difficult to master for children with cerebral palsy because of kinesthesia. This is characterized by a lack of sensation in the hands and fingers that hampers the bodily motions needed for writing. It is also difficult to learn cursive writing correctly when letters or syllables must be pronounced as one writes them. Children who do not have the oral motor ability to say a "b" as it is being written are at a disadvantage.

I found that this subject is best taught as a skill with games and puzzles, and by the teacher who works willingly at the chalkboard, "spoon feeding" the skills visually for the children.

I believe it is as easy to teach big words as well as little words like *cat, dog, pig*. The big words have more clues as you keep building on the same roots and phonetic clusters. Whenever possible, I introduced larger words and made certain that pronunciation was correct as well as the meaning, whenever possible.

I devised a kind of game I played at the chalkboard with them. Those without speech had a way of beating the time to each syllable It was fun, but a tremendous task for the teacher. One of my favorites was *antidisestablishmentarianism*. The children learned to pronounce this word like a song with syllables.

One of my students went home to find a neighborhood electrician working at her house. This is how their conversation went:

He: "How's school?"
She: "Fine".
He: "What's your favorite subject?"
She: "Spelling."
Then she threw him a question.
She: "Can you spell antidisestablishmentarianism? I can."
What could he say?

There was much ado about silent letters in words and the use of memory for spelling. There were tricks to remember, like writing *bag*, then *dad* with an *h* between them, making *Baghdad*.

There is no rest for the teacher when so much teaching needed to be spoon-fed at the chalkboard.

There is concern about technology for the teacher these days with computers that spell and process words.

Will our handwriting eventually become illegible from lack of use? Will anything be "handwritten with love?" Will math skills become obsolete and handwriting so archaic that is will have to be rediscovered as a kinetic art!

Children with handicaps, like all children, love to write, to hold a pencil or crayon, reproducing what they have learned. This speeds the learning process. Yet they may still write with difficulty.

For example, see the letter from Paula at the end of the photo section on page 64. At first glance, it is difficult to read, but the thoughts it communicates are precious and real.

Mathematics

My combined third and fourth grade class had heard about mathematics. I was overwhelmed with the problems entailed with teaching this subject but there was no time for fear, doubts and stress.

I had no alternative except to expose them to the necessary academic work and see how it went. One must work to bring excitement to the children in difficult situations like this. Those with good hand dexterity and with the needed faculties intact were no problem, but the children with cerebral palsy, possessing average or above average intelligence but with impaired physical ability, would need special attention much of the time.

Without functional speech and manual dexterity, they would instead have to learn shapes, sizes, and amounts by playing with concrete materials on their desks. This helped them develop curiosity about numbers and provided a foundation for concepts of abstract reasoning.

Then they needed help to build confidence in using numbers daily. There was a limit to progress for some children with cerebral palsy, while others were able to use numbers normally in everyday life and at grade level.

For some, it was difficult to convey even a taste for mathematics. Much of the time I was at the chalkboard (one of the oldest visual aids for teaching) for illustration and demonstration. In time, the overhead projector became an excellent device as a visual aid. I had taken the bull by the horns and there was no alternative but to fight. The overhead projector was perfect for a child lying on a plinth.

The children loved number facts and the games we invented to awaken their interest. The commercial cards featuring number facts had each child's level in color. The entire class participated in games regardless of level. I kept a careful record of each child's progress.

Each pack contained 25 cards making a perfect score possible. Individual children were tested on their own level. There was no "flashing" of cards but, (language being important), each child was questioned orally and in turn by a reader. For instance:

"How many are 4 plus 5?"

"Four plus five make nine." (Answering in complete sentences improved language use and understanding.)

For more advanced levels, the scores were tracked cumulatively, producing an index of individual yearly progress for each child. Seeing the progress was motivation enough for any teacher.

Always there are exceptional children who can do more; these were given bigger challenges. Some, for example, read the number facts as a question in Spanish. For instance:

"Quantos hacen dos y dos?"

"Dos y dos hacen quatro."

"Quantos hacen cinco menos tres?"

"Cinco menos tres hacen dos."

"Quantos hacen dos por tres?"

"Dos por tres hacen seis."

"Quantos hacen cuatro dividio por dos?"

"Cuatro dividio por dos hacen dos."

Our orthopedic classes at #5 and #29 Schools in Rochester were demonstration classes observed by various visitors including education students, teachers and administrators, from areas near and far. If I had time to be concerned it would be over the fact that I felt I was running a continual "Open House." Interest was running high in this new area of teaching.

I taught my 3rd and 4th grade classes Spanish and had them enact "The Three Little Pigs" or "Los Tres Cerditos." While practicing, they were doing their best but not quite getting into the spirit of things, so I began to exhort them a little too loudly, "Come on, you're not acting like pigs. *You're pigs! **Act like PIGS!***"

Thanks to the open door, I was heard up and down the hall.

The Spanish class was delightful. The children learned incidentally as a baby first learns to listen, and then eventually speaks. I had marvelous language cassettes and played them everyday during arrival, playtime, lunch and dismissal as if it were background music. Their ears became attuned to the sound.

Because I taught both 3rd and 4th grade children, the 3rd grade received two entire years of the Spanish language and the 4th grade, one year. There was listening, speaking and reading Spanish, but absolutely no writing as babies do not write until ready, and English was always a priority.

A group of South American educators was one of the most prestigious groups we entertained. They were amazed at the perfect Spanish we taught, comparing it to Shakespearean English (and therefore not exactly what you would hear on the street). This was not to my credit but to the very select cassette collections we used.

Our Latino visitors became so excited that in appreciation, they handed each child a Spanish coin. Then with heartfelt "Adios, amigos," they departed.

I congratulated the children, but then I noticed one sad face. It was John Joseph, a boy with muscular dystrophy, whom the visitors missed. He had not received a coin. This was not right. I quickly dashed into the corridor, apprehended the group and holding out my hand declared, "Sorry, you missed one child."

The visitors' small change was already exhausted, so John Joseph received the biggest and most valuable coin.

Things You Can't Do Anymore

I wrote previously about the pleasant, spacious dining room for the children at #5 School, including three sizes of tables, chairs to match and space for wheelchairs. Lunch time was quiet, peaceful, relaxing and happy. The adults in charge of the procession to the dining room had to take care because many children walked independently with difficulty.

For many years before I arrived, the children and staff said "Grace" before meals. It was a lovely tradition of praying before eating: "Bless this food for our use and us to Thy service."

Then the day came in the early 1960's when public schools were disallowed this choice. The children looked to teachers for a reason. We simply suggested a silent blessing, each in his own way. Children are so resilient. In a few days this practice hit the New Age – scary in some ways.

However, there are ways of handling all situations. Somehow hope, fun, good humor and, above all, love for one another can all be filtered into the school situation. We continued to strive for this daily.

Stephen, with spina bifida, used crutches and was not a fast walker, but, nevertheless, a delightfully fast talker in his wheelchair. He was academically above grade level, a handsome 10 year old who made friends, and who remembered and loved them. He was "like some, like all, like no other one."

I recall the day Franklin arrived at school. He immediately fell into conversation with others and I could overhear him talking about preparing for First Communion. Franklin said, "Catholics are not supposed to steal."

Stephen jumped in, "Not just Catholics; nobody is supposed to steal, that's a commandment. Miss Teach, what is the greatest commandment?" (Believe me, this was a command, not a question).

I answered "The Lord our God is one Lord and you must love the Lord your God with all your heart, with all your soul, with all your mind and with all your strength and the second is like unto this: you must love your neighbor as yourself." *(With apologies to Matthew 22: 37-39.)*

The door was open and Stephen again spoke "That's right." There wasn't a sound or shadow near the door. There is no door that could keep God out.

Stephen was an unforgettable representative of all the little boys in our Orthopedic Dept. One day, he unpacked his book bag, removing a crucifix on a standard and placed it on his desk.

I asked him about it and he responded that whenever he tells his neighbor something nice, "she gives it to me." It was a blessing for two days on his desk.

We also heard countless stories of Stephen's outdoor games with neighborhood children as he played via his wheelchair. One time a football was unavailable. He reluctantly allowed his teddy bear to be tossed about in rough play. It landed high in a tree.

Before bedtime the Rochester Fire Department came to the rescue (Well, perhaps it was an off-duty member of the fire department who came to the rescue and not the whole department). But I believed Stephen.

At his funeral a few years later, the bear was close by.

Typical Attendant Learnings

I remember two 8-year-old sports reporters, Larry, with cerebral palsy, and Tom, with spina bifida. Both were prime third graders. They could stand straight and were blessed with excellent speech proving positively that a physical disability is not an impediment unless it prevents one from succeeding in a chosen career.

No motivation was necessary, on my part, to encourage these little boys to read the newspapers as homework and to select news details and prepare independently for a report to their classmates each morning. The excitement was contagious and attendant learnings for the report to classmates were great.

However, the vocabulary of baseball wasn't the most literary when you consider results being reported in words like "annihilated, blanked out, slaughtered and zeroed" as teams lost throughout the U.S. This was in the early 1960's but our reporters knew events from the late 1950's that were topical for them to report.

They knew that Mickey Mantle led the American League in home runs for three years and that Willie Mays did the same in the National League in the early '60's, becoming one of baseball's most famous outfielders. Larry and Tom reported on the story of Jackie Robinson which happened years before their time.

We chuckled over their knowledge of Yogi Berra, most valuable player in the mid-50's, who was called "Yogi" because he resembled a Hindu practicing yoga as he sat viewing a movie. They tickled the ears of their classmates with their stories.

As a 3rd grader, Larry was serious as he spoke. He looked and acted like a small size CEO. Tom was more mellow. I remember a discussion one day concerning the expression "guts." Larry absolutely declined to use another word such as "determination" or "fortitude," and would agree to nothing like "grace under pressure"!

With the open door of our classroom we never knew who was in the audience in the corridor to overhear us, and "guts" was not exactly a study word in our curriculum.

There are other happenings that haunt me. The sports report was followed by the Pledge of Allegiance, true, solemn and serious, and then followed by a patriotic song.

At this, I felt betrayed. There were several singers in the class who could have supported me. Instead, I was the soloist – as off-key and breathless as Edith Bunker in "All in the Family." Now, I do agree that teaching children should be a open profession; thus the door of my classroom was always open for public display -- even for my humble attempts at singing.

One of my favorite memories is a gift of a flower almost too beautiful to be true. It was a huge pink and white peony in full bloom and so large that it looked like the grandmother of all peonies.

Carol, age eight, blond, beautiful, bright eyed and giggly, was excited to bring such a gift to "Miss Teach." An aide helped her to the center of the floor space and left her.

I was looking in another direction but my peripheral vision told me there was something exciting in store. Carol's involuntary athetoid trembling started and increased until every petal of the flower left its base and fluttered to the floor in a perfect circle surrounding her.

She was left with only the tall green stem in her hand.

My sixth sense told me to say, "Don't move, Carol."

We lifted her out of the circle of fresh pink and white petals, explaining simultaneously that she had created a lovely authentic Japanese floral arrangement of fresh petals on the floor. Carol remained peaceful and the petals held their design on the floor all day. The green stem lasted a week in a vase of water on my desk.

It was a declaration. It was Carol's gift, an opportunity for all of us to learn, and it remains in my mind's eye to this day as a crystal clear memory.

The Challenge of Teaching Teens

I WAS FORTUNATE in teaching all levels of elementary grades but my appreciation of each level did not come suddenly. The primary through fourth grade was challenging enough but the next level required even more adaptation on my part.

The young teenagers were gentle, serious, fierce, energetic and helpful, but possessed a shortage of good judgment and tact. Teenagers think they are adults and dealing with them calls for constant energy on the part of teachers and parents. My belief had always been that young teenagers should come before "Head Starters" in line for federal and state financial assistance and all it entails.

However, teens at this level soon became my favorites, and as young adults, were capable of both understanding and enthusiasm. They became my teaching staff as they assisted one another in the classroom. Those with speech were allowed to speak out in class at any time, provided they learned not to interrupt tactlessly.

Propriety was taught and learned without breaking their spirit. I often heard a child's voice unconsciously humming a popular tune, "You go to my head like a rolly coaster ride!"

There is little to add concerning academic work at this level. The subject content in the 1950's progressed in all areas with basics, even bedrock basics, relearned and reviewed as needed for children who had gaps in their educational progress, as is often found in cerebral palsy cases. Some with multiple handicaps, which might never be overcome, had to be continually "spoon-fed" or tutored for advancement to junior high school.

Testing was scheduled from time to time to ascertain their mental ability. Always it was necessary to teach commensurate with their mental age. Elsa Haussermann's study on Stanford-Binet testing of children with cerebral palsy certainly confirms this.

The curriculum was gauged to a standard of need and fitness for each individual child and the teacher simply had to establish a standard that could be sustained. It is surprising how many students could evolve and succeed in spite of multiple disabilities and the unusual methods of teaching required.

Teaching plans consisted of reading, mathematics, language arts, social studies, science, music, physical education and art. Reading was most important and was taught and coordinated in all the above studies. Learning to read was most imperative for the handicapped, because of the impediments involved in their make-up and their physical inactivity.

Reading materials, devices, colorful books, films, tapes and every possible item that would spark the love of books, had to be on hand. I guarded against too much television and films in school because the reader could profit more by forming his own pictures in his mind. I wish that all movies and TV episodes could be captioned with adequate space for the printed word. This would be a boon to the teaching of reading.

Using games and other practical tools was the only way to teach mathematics, since the students' experience and manipulative skills have often been delayed. My groups enjoyed games of playing, writing and computing and liked to spend hours with this method.

Without paper or pencil we were obliged to use the math text as a reading lesson when dealing with reasoning problems. I used the chalkboard for demonstrating number solutions.

Because the children had such poor hand use, I found that lecture with demonstration at the chalkboard was the method that was most rewarding and enjoyable It also caused less tension and stress.

My art left much to be desired and made for much laughter, but produced reasonable results in learning and reduced the need for devices and gadgets that the children's hands could not have managed.

Language arts was an ongoing concern from the pupils' arrival at school to dismissal time, since constant practice, oral and written, was necessary for speech therapy. Enrichment through the careful selection of books for the children, read to them by the teacher, was the right path.

Grammar is another difficult subject to teach. Verbose people, using incorrect language, are often imitated and copied even by good listeners. We wrestled and had fun with everyday inaccuracies. Here are a few (with corrections):

"Him and me are going" (He and I are going)
"Give it to you and I" (Give it to you and me)
"They coming is good" (Their coming is good)

These common mistakes are made and even defended by educators occasionally. They argue that if what is meant or intended is clear, the grammar can often be over-looked. However, learners need to know the truth and to learn proper grammar. Intellectual honesty and accountability should be required of the teacher.

One of my methods, which is rare today, was to diagram sentences. The children loved and understood it. Doesn't it make sense, in this world of technology, where everything is pictured, filmed, charted, diagrammed and analyzed, with Power Point slides and a whole cable TV channel dedicated to stock market charts, that the English sentence should deserve this same attention?

As I taught, I pondered the question of discipline based on the need for order in learning. I was strict as to proper behavior. "Three strikes" was not my approach to tolerance in those days.

Misbehavior, discourtesy and failure to work hard were not tolerated despite the prevalence of handicaps, but were discussed and corrected, if possible, immediately. Drill and practice were right and proper for all, especially for those who have difficulty with orienta-

ı time and space as found in children with cerebral palsy. Rep-
n of correct language was necessary for the establishment of the neural bond. This was hard work mentally and physically, causing fatigue. I often reminded the children from time to time that life was tough and they understood this. I held them to this standard as long as they had average to above average intelligence and the desire to succeed. This periodically gave rise to tension and stress for teachers as well as pupils. Thankfully, they were always followed by words like "OK, let's begin again."

I remember being on duty for lunch period one day trying to keep order. After the handicapped children were seated at tables, a group of regulars from the second floor joined them. This was a mutual, friendly get-together for both groups. Jack, who had spina bifida, was popular and loved by the "regulars," who breezed into the dining room in perfect marching formation each day. They all greeted Jack individually with "Hi Jack – Hi Jack" several times.

One day I shouted an order and commanded "There will be no 'hi-jacking' here today!" There followed the roar of laughter. We all won. Lunch was delicious. There was a kind of release of tension, causing a more restful picture.

On one occasion I remember struggling with hope and faith that Bill, a brilliant young man with multiple physical handicaps, would respond correctly to test questions, proving that he was knowledgeable in the subject. He indicated correctly with the use of the conversation board, by pointing to the answers with the knuckles of one hand while I recorded his answers. I was able to vouch for his high intelligence.

The sequel is that I had promised to dance for him if he persevered, which he did. The classroom runner sped to the corridor and shouted, "Miss Teach is dancing, Miss Teach is dancing!"

I recall considering various methods to teach the orthopedically disabled children effectively. Their problems were mostly physical and mechanical. They were non-ambulatory and had poor hand use with various speech disorders. This put tremendous pressure on a teacher's responsibility to vouch objectively for the pupil's grade level and achievement.

I even harked back for ideas to Bessie Griffin, an outstanding teacher from my 8th grade in the 1930's. Hers was a self-contained classroom with forty students, completely scholastic and none were visibly handicapped. I don't recall even a minor disciplinary case in a year. "Leo" was allowed to rest his head on the desk and take a daily nap because he arose at 4 am every day to deliver milk in town.

Miss Griffin was brilliant, an "orator" in all areas of education and generous in spreading her talents. She always gave us clearly defined instructions and consistently kept us busy and disciplined. Structured work was at the heart of her approach to discipline in learning.

At intervals, if we tired, she ordered a "break" to ease tension and would lead us in a sing-a-long. Her favorites were songs by Stephen Foster that she knew from childhood. How I loved "Old Black Joe" and cried for him! The following, her favorite, I write now from memory:

The Old Oaken Bucket

How dear to my heart are the scenes of my childhood
When fond recollections present them to view
The old oaken bucket, the iron-bound bucket
The moss-covered bucket that hung in the well.

We loved this song. Can you imagine teenagers today singing this song? Perhaps only for history class.

It would be great to emulate Miss Griffin even in the least of her values, and in her principles and love for teaching.

There is No End to Learning

I don't want to overemphasize the differences in teaching physically disabled children from the able-bodied. They have much in common, but the differences are significant too. Enjoyable and satisfying as teaching children with disabilities is, the work is exhausting and stressful because of the demands of accountability.

The teacher is required to be on the alert constantly, use time profitably, plan for emergencies, be ready for interruptions, and meet a demanding schedule for physical, occupational and speech therapies. In the mid 1950's, aid-raid drills were practiced but were actually simpler than fire drills because taking the elevator from the 3rd floor was allowed. The air-raid drills took us to the half dug-out basement of #5 School.

There were also assembly programs with the regular school population. It was a blessing to our department to be able to join others in regular school activities on holiday occasions and in performances of concerts and plays.

Our children also joined the "regulars" in Unit Activity projects for social growth. This was exciting, time consuming and hard work physically for the teacher. What can be more appropriate than a Courtesy Campaign, a unit of fun for the entire school? I remember it well! Because children with cerebral palsy had difficulty speaking, I waited for every lip movement signifying "please" . . . "thank you" . . . "may I" . . . "you're welcome."

I will never forget one day of the campaign when I dropped my pencil and two competitive boys in wheelchairs slid to the floor to retrieve the pencil for me. Of course, their courtesy was recognized and appreciated, but a half-hour elapsed before the boys could be lifted back into their chairs and work resumed. Mt. Everest had been climbed that "Week of Courtesy!"

Class enrollment

Class size is paramount in setting up a viable learning situation for orthopedically handicapped children. Provided mental age is proven average, four multiply-disabled children could make up one class. In planning, we might multiply each child by the number of his handicaps, such as paralysis, low muscle tone, lack of coordination, deafness, vision impairment, etc. So the four children could actually become the equivalent of perhaps 16 total enrollment for that one class. Even then, a teacher would need a tutor, aide or volunteer. I recall one year having twenty children in a class, selectively placed but moderately handicapped and of average intelligence.

No administration can make up a class for a teacher without listing carefully and thoroughly every case. Accountability by the teacher for each child is paramount. In Rochester, we faced the situation and our administrators were understanding and knowledgeable concerning the psychology of the handicapped. The Junior Guild for Crippled Children, Inc., of Rochester, NY was one of our indispensible sources of assistance.

The Teacher's Desk

During my teacher training, I had visited various schools to observe the work of experts. To me, the positive plans and ideas were so overwhelming that I needed to hitch my wagon to a star and then get out and push. There was one outstanding idea for me - my desk would not be a watchtower. I would not and could not sit while my children performed "seatwork" alone at their desks. However there was one time of day when I was forced to sit at my desk. It was 9 a.m. arrival time.

Aides helped with outdoor wraps, with books, money for weekly lunches, notes to the teacher. Children who needed a short conference or interview waited in line for me. The following are several of these spontaneous interviews.

♦ *Bert announced* that his dad helped with homework the night before, and added "But I need to whisper this to you; *my dad has poison ivy*." We discussed it briefly and cleared up the fact that this was neither fatal nor contagious.

♦ *Jenna, a classic beauty,* and an elegant sixth grader, reported about a meeting she had attended the night before for girls with problems of great concern. Her question to the speaker was "Will I ever be married?" After the discussion, the leader said. "Someday you are likely to meet a man of quality who will take care of you." Several years later, that promise came true and she had a truly beautiful wedding.

♦ *A boy reported* that his little brother started kindergarten that day. Since children were asked to give their name and tell where they lived on the first day of school, his father had instructed him to say "I'm Freddie the Frog and I live under a rock!"

♦ *Debbie was next in line.* Even in the 1950's, teachers were not allowed to hug a child. No legislation or spoken order could change my actions then, or now, at her story about an incident at home involving her puppy, which is even now too painful to write about. All I could do was hug her and hold her until she was quiet.

♦ *After studying phonetics,* David did voluntary homework. In the morning, he reported to me that there was a "th" in his pocket. Can you imagine me going through his tiny bluejean pockets looking for that "th"?

♦ *Harry was last in line* for a short interview that day and looked down at me, as I sat at my desk waiting for him to talk. He was a tall sixth grader, not academically swift, but courteous, observant and alert. His handicaps were serious but not visible. Hesitant to speak, he smiled and I waited for him to utter a word or two.

My class was quietly busy with the help of aides. Some were evidently completing previous projects and I had trained them to wait, be patient, and occupy themselves somehow during my interviews. The sun shone brightly on my desk as I sat waiting for Harry to speak momentarily. It was a beautiful, serene day and I was in no hurry.

The large windows faced North Plymouth Avenue. The sun's rays were glorious, comfortable, restful, and I remember allowing myself seconds of relaxation. Still Harry remained smiling and silent while gazing straight at my head.

Perhaps he noticed my hair in the sunshine, I thought. My mother had often remarked how the sun caused my hair to mix and blend into different shades of red, brown and blond. (Please excuse my lack of humility).

My tranquillity abruptly came to an end as I heard Harry say, "Miss Teach, I see you are growing a mustache."

IN THE EARLY 1950's there was good news concerning research into the causes and possible cures for poliomyelitis and muscular dystrophy. Great strides were made against polio with the development of a vaccine for injection by Dr. Jonas Salk in 1955 and by Dr. Albert Sabin who developed an oral vaccine to prevent polio. Muscular dystrophy was just beginning to receive attention and serious research.

By 1976, there were eight muscular dystrophy cases in our department and no polio cases. I remember George, the last student with polio to enter #5 School. He arrived braced from head to foot with arms and hands that responded perfectly to his crutches as he walked. Only his head and neck were free of braces. Handsome he was with a brain that raced far ahead of the curriculum.

It was 2nd grade when he first came to my class, and later he was mainstreamed in his district public school. His grading for academic progress was no problem. His reading ability and his fluency with words was exceptional. Beginners often read just words, while he fluently read whole phrases with expression.

I recall how he introduced himself in my 2nd grade. He said, "When I was in kindergarten, I could dash with the speed of a deer across my grandfather's daisy field!"

What imagery!

Muscular dystrophy was and is the most difficult disability for me even to consider because of the long, patient road necessary to even hope for relief and cure. It is a road dotted with a constant succession of trial and error, success and failure on the part of doctors and therapists, parents and teachers. Traveling it takes patience and hard work. John Joseph took me on that road.

He entered my class as a handsome little boy, dressed in bib overalls. As a seven year old, he walked with an unusual gait for a child, like a soldier on parade with a dignity which I could not understand. I did not know his diagnosis, since I had not yet read his case history. He had muscular dystrophy and was always careful as well as fearful of falling.

I felt he needed a wheelchair at times, but the medical staff usually forestalled or delayed using a wheelchair, trying to save muscles, bones and joints from weakening from non-use. My position was to take orders. I wanted the child at peace and safe to enjoy life. I favored him to prevent falls.

John Joseph was aware at an early age of his problems. Through the media he heard all kinds of information about muscular dystrophy, while not knowing the vocabulary.

He entered the classroom one morning, stood in the doorway and announced, "I'm not going to survive."

This was an attitude we would have to work on. John Joseph became an avid reader, making this skill a precious gift to him then and later.

It is impossible to tell how many times a day he fell, but, through excellent therapy, he could get up independently.

This is how he did it. (Reader, try this!):

1. Turn over on the floor and lie on your stomach in a prone position.

2. Get up on your hands and knees.

3. With hands on the floor, raise your buttocks high until your legs are stiff and straight up.

4. "Walk" your hands back to your feet and proceed up the rest of the body to a standing position.

This routine, however, was short-lived. I continued to disagree with the orders to have him walk independently. John was growing tall and heavy as a teenager. He could no longer follow the above directions and I could no longer lift him. And although I disagreed with the medical staff, I could appreciate their reasoning in delaying the use of a wheelchair.

I searched for some solution to ease the situation, believing that "there is a way of solving every case."

The department provided help when possible, but you had to call for help. However, I could not leave the class and, unless there was a runner in my class, we often waited.

We did not have a classroom phone. The technology was on its way, to be sure. Meanwhile, John Joseph was on the floor.

There was a solution to this situation. I allowed the children who could walk to sit with John Joseph on the floor. Those remaining in wheelchairs, circled around him and we continued the lessons. We had a ball! This procedure went on for months.

Finally he had done enough falling and was granted a wheelchair. I saw the expression on his face when he was lifted into it. He had won comfort and safety from falling. *Alleluia!*

The morning after earning his wheelchair, John Joseph rolled in on those blessed wheels. He had the attention of everyone in view as he held his open palm up in a blessing and said, "Peace be to you."

John Joseph was happy sitting in his chair on wheels. He enjoyed reading and progressed in all academic learnings, except in some subjects like math, when he could no longer hold a pencil. In his own way he was a pioneer "like some, like all, like no other".

Parents of Handicapped Children

The word *parent* itself is too basic a word to be used to describe the great overflow of good characteristics needed by mothers and fathers who care for and educate their children. They are the first teachers and their children's greatest advocates.

Community and state meetings should make conscious efforts to hear the problems of these advocates and to learn from them. We also need their help and support in promoting the care and education of children and insisting on periodic testing to measure mental ability in terms of chronological age so that each child can be assured of having educational materials commensurate with his mental age.

Until a child enters a school program, parents of a multiply-handicapped child are on twenty-four hour duty at home, a tremendous job even with every kind of aid. Ordinary daily routines must be carried on in extraordinary ways for their children.

Compatible parents living harmoniously and sharing the daily routine with love are necessary for a handicapped child's daily program. These are priceless gifts both for themselves and for their entire family.

Accomplishments in growth are slow and often imperceptible. A child's leisure time and entertainment, when vision, hearing and poor hand use are diminished to any degree, can be a source of discord in the family. Parents who have to support a child with a disability are twice as likely as other parents to split up.

A handicapped child growing up in a typical home with siblings and organized, capable parents will learn through caring, sharing, fighting and cooperating. The whole family will become wiser and stronger and more capable if they remain open to the challenges that handicaps present and enjoy the support that the school and their community owes them.

Changes in disability and education legislation since I was teaching have had a tremendous impact. But the parents and the child still need the personal interest and concern of the teachers.

I recall a parent-child case when I first entered work with the handicapped in the public schools in Rochester. I needed help in September, teaching a third grader named Jerry who had spina bifida. His cumulative record in June simply stated, "He is a good boy."

Young and hoping for help, I raised my eyebrows, which helped open my eyes, and of course agreed with his former teacher. However, this excellent pioneer teacher had retired that year and I could not consult her.

Parents love and care for the children but are not paid for their "homework." I had as many conferences with parents as I or they requested and drew from them an honest pleasure in learning and planning for their child. I had to learn to relate to them as unpaid professional partners who shared my commitment to education.

Even when I disagreed with them psychologically I did not let this interfere with our shared commitment to progress. Instead, I acknowledged their level of frustration. Tentative agreement can bring much peace to a sad situation.

Then I tried to raise the level.

I remember Jerry's mother sitting with me one day. She cried a river of tears for ten minutes using a whole box of Kleenex tissues that was within arm's reach. We kept boxes of them at handy places around the classroom for me and the aides to care for runaway noses where hands were nonfunctioning. One should have empathy for people who can cry openly for good reason.

At third grade level, her son was unhappy, angry, argumentative and uncommunicative with little self-esteem. From the waist down he was completely disabled. Using crutches, his arms and shoulders bore the weight of a plump body that was visibly heavy.

Jerry held his chronological age level academically, but there was fear he would become discouraged and lose enthusiasm for learning. He was too seriously aware of his different appearance. The orthopedic department of #5 School and caring parents together cleared his case for reasonable progress.

There is a sequel to the above story which proved Jerry's enthusiasm for education. My research and memory of him helped.

In my work at Edith Hartwell Clinic in 1949, I remember Jerry as a 4-year-old preschooler in that schoolroom I described earlier. It was the teakwood paneled living room in the mansion in LeRoy.

With the head nurse, I remember sitting in a corner discussing children available for kindergarten class. Jerry was playing with a small group of preschoolers at the far end of the room, diagonally away from us.

Hearing his name being mentioned, Jerry "swam" across that room on his belly and landed at my feet. He obviously knew something about what we were planning. I can never forget his enthusiasm. I listed him for the kindergarten class.

He and his caring parents never lost this enthusiasm for learning. Today he is an accountant.

Parents should be compatible and work on building a happy family life at home, taking advantages of private and public help for their handicapped child. I enjoyed the fun and laughter that often came from home to school.

One morning during our two to three minute interviews, Jackie lowered his voice to share with me his father's remark concerning his report card, feeling he should give me fair warning. "My dad said, if the next report card did not improve, someone would be spanked."

I wondered for a moment: *Could that someone be me?*

Parents and teachers are responsible for the adults of tomorrow. This is a profound human responsibility and we should know that, after we rest following all the tension in this necessary work, the softest pillow is a clear conscience.

Besides Head Start which receives a federal grant, we need mentoring and tutoring for young teens to address problems early. It is imperative that we also have programs to educate parents.

The last parent education course we had in Rochester, N.Y., in the early 1950's, was discontinued around 1980. The director was Mae Mattson, a true educator. These classes were successful and those in #5 School were excellent.

If a system works, administrators should keep it going, not declare it obsolete, regardless of cost. People do not change basically, children learn the same way at any age and at any time.

There is much to say about easing the work of parents.

I did not prescribe homework for handicapped children, except for reading books. It is common sense that children with handicaps work hard. They ride buses, have daily therapy, and school itself can be exhausting for them. Lessons should be covered in school and not delegated to homework for parents to oversee. Children and families should have a chance to relax in the evening.

Teachers should visit the homes of their pupils at least once a year to ascertain their needs. Parents are the first and continual teachers of their children, as are all who share information and help as neighbors and friends. People in all areas of life are constantly instructing with information and direction for those in their path.

I remember Michael, a preschooler with muscular dystrophy, who sadly did not have long to live. He came to me in a wheelchair. He was a big man of a boy, and spoke fluently but rarely. He paid attention, listened to instructions with interest, using proper facial expressions. He was learning.

One day at dismissal time, I helped him with wraps for the trip home. His excitement was high and he asked that I hurry. He wanted to get home to "watch the cat." Such a nice, soft, furry animal, I thought, because a house is not a home without a cat.

I planned to visit his parents that week. I arrived at his house minutes before his bus and watched as he arrived home, to see his cat. But I couldn't figure out why his mother was rushing about.

She had a large picture window open where she hurried to place his wheelchair so that he could look out the window.

That's when I noticed. There, as if on a stage, was a huge Caterpillar tractor equipped on each side with continuous belts over cogged wheels. It moved over rough ground and dug the good earth as Mike watched through his window. *That was his "cat".*

The operator wore a hard hat as did all the workers and Michael watched their every move. The project was super homework for Mike.

His mother recognized this as Michael's window on the world, while the Cat's hard-hat operators and his teacher provided a living textbook on the subject of earth-moving and engineering. They were his teachers. He was studying the work of an engineer thanks to his parents' positive insights.

I remember standing near a table in the orthopedic children's dining room as an aide fed a child her home packed lunch. Each item of food was wrapped attractively and unwrapped ceremoniously by the aide. A note from the child's mother was enclosed which the aide carefully opened and read, "I love you, Kim."

Now that is the kind of lesson only a loving parent can teach.

Parents need an overflow of good characteristics. They need to be an example to their children to demonstrate the importance of work as well as the value of the joys and sorrows of life which mix and blend into the colors of which happiness is made.

These are the most important lessons of all.

Student Teachers

It was my pleasure to supervise student teachers at #5 and #29 Schools in Rochester. All were from N.Y. State University College for Teachers in Buffalo.

I don't recall the length of their course (perhaps 6 months) but, no matter, it was their accomplishments that were important.

The students who were the most successful were those who felt comfortable about themselves, about other people, and were able to meet the demands of their own lives. This knowledge of them was a help to me in grading them. I demanded their best in participation in the learning process for multiply-handicapped children since a well thought out rationale was essential. Some teachers are blessed with pure common sense, but shouldn't this be true of all teaching?

Teachers must study and learn before taking charge. There are no rehearsals. All you ever do is a mere shadow of your full potential, but you must execute it well. A good rationale for using a method is essential and it must prove itself in the process.

I was strict about student plans. I remember insisting that one of my students not plan to make paper hats for a birthday party because experience told me that a sky-piece won't stay on the head of a child with cerebral palsy.

However, this particular student insisted on making the hats. I demanded proof and the next day, she reported, "Last night, I made a paper hat, fastened it on my head, turned somersaults on my bed, and the hat stayed." I conceded the point. She had done her homework and made an effort to prove her approach. Congratulations to her clownship! We often acted like clowns.

Student teachers were also graded on their interest and respect for people and on their willingness and ability to work hard continuously to prove that no one ever knows what he can't do.

At the risk of being negative, I always stressed: If you don't like what you are doing . . . if you don't love the people around you . . . if you don't believe in common sense . . . if you aren't definite about what you do . . . you may be courting disaster for yourself and for the children.

These children have had a life experience beyond their years. If you don't think you have the ability to work with them, then act as if you do and you will begin to learn. A handicapped child can teach us to appreciate the ability we have to move beyond our limitations and to reach our full potential by helping others reach theirs.

I found it necessary for teachers of disabled children to be certified in methods of education as well as liberal arts and also important for them to minor in art or music. The former is excellent prepa-ration for explaining and demonstrating in lecture-type lessons where the learner has only his vision and hearing and is taught with the help of a chalkboard. Ability to perform music, at whatever level, is also a wonderful remedy for stress and tension.

One always needs empathy for others in working with disabled or sick people. Empathy is a projection of one's own personality into the personality of another in order to understand him better, a way of identifying with them and seeing things from their perspective. And that is a prerequisite to reaching and teaching them.

In dealing with disabled children or adults, it is also important not to intellectualize too deeply. I believe it might slow up the job!

Like a sonata in music, teaching is exposition, development, recapitulation. The same is true in academics where you have verbal-ization and symbolization.

Even now I am cognizant of the success of many of my student teachers and am proud of my association with them.

Legislation is not the whole answer for our children nor is money. Let's not blame the times.

Children learn as they have always learned. Far more serious is lack of discipline, respect, generosity, love, and empathy for our neighbor. The richest and finest schools that money can buy cannot survive on money alone. Without love and discipline they will fail.

There are times when every teacher feels discouragement, and I was no exception. I found healing in laughter and fun, and by re-maining thankful for the many blessings I received in teaching dis-abled children. At times like this, they were the instructors and I was the pupil to be disciplined by learning from their example how to ac-cept rejection, inconvenience, and problems of health or sorrow. I learned that with the right attitude, I could turn each of these into happiness daily.

To this day, I believe firmly there is no end to learning.

The Students Speak

LIKE ALL TEACHERS, after years of teaching I have collected a number of notes and letters from students and parents. Most are spontaneous thank you notes, some are friendly and newsy, all touch the teacher's heart. Here are excerpts from some of them:

* * *

"Last week we heard from the school district that Bobby has been chosen for the Major Achievement Program (MAP) for fifth grade this fall. We were all delighted and thought how this justified your confidence in his ability last spring. . . . While this is unquestionably a great tribute to Bobby's abilities, both intellectual and emotional, we realize how great was your contribution to his educational success. That year he spent in your class was certainly one of his happiest and most productive, and established a pattern of success which was such an important asset to him in a new school." (1971)

* * *

"Your wonderful letter is placed among my treasures. . . . My son was so fond of you and you were such a good teacher and friend to him. . . . The presence of Stephen in our home for ten years was a wonderful blessing. We gained much in spiritual strength, and learned the true meaning of joy and sorrow . . . . as well as patience, understanding and appreciation. He probably influenced more lives for good in his short lifetime than many others do in fourscore years." (1955)

* * *

"You are good for the soul! Your teaching has deep beauty." *(from the school principal!)*

"Dear Miss Remis: I like you very much. I very glad I had you this year too. You are just as good this year as you were last year. I have larned a lot from you in two years. You are a very nice person. I will miss you very much nexted year. But I will still see you maybe in the luch rom, halls or in the office." (1970)

* * *

"The other day while we were reviewing for the American Studies Regents (examination), the teacher wanted to know who said the famous words "Walk softly and carry a big stick" and I thought to myself "Miss Remis and Teddy Roosevelt". (1978)

* * *

In the photo section of this book there is a picture of a letter written in crayon by a young girl with cerebral palsy. This labor of love reads: "Teacher of the Year. To a teacher who has helped me and care for me and gave me critacism and has been kind . From Paula." (1975)

* * *

Many volunteer aides from the Rochester Guild for Crippled Children, Inc., helped in the classroom, tutoring the children and taking them to the school library. On December 18, 1972, the children and I had a breakfast party for them and our student teacher. The children wrote thank you letters to Mrs. Smith, Mrs. Hill and Mrs. Carlson. All contributed their sentiments to the letters, which one child then typed. The letters express the children's thanks for "trips to the Library, help with number facts, being around when we need help, and for the books you gave us."

The letters also have a line addressed to the husbands: "Thank you Mr. X for letting Mrs. X come on Mondays."

* * *

In many a teacher's life, there is a student whose friendship endures beyond the classroom and transcends roles of teacher and student. I received a letter from Andrea Levy when I was about to retire.

She had been my student in P.S. #29 in an ungraded elementary class. My correspondence with her later continued through her college career, graduate school, and into her career as a school social worker. For most of our correspondence, I was "Dear Miss Remis." Later, when she was out of school and established in a career, I became simply "Dear Anne." Here are excerpts from a few of her letters:

* * *

"First, there are the examples you set for all your students. I cannot remember a teacher who taught me so much about attitudes toward people and how they result in others returning respect and courtesy toward yourself. Secondly, there is your patience. I do not once remember your being short, or losing your temper with any of your students. Your warm and encouraging words and kind smile were enough to urge us on through the most difficult periods. I think perhaps I owe my own perseverance in my studies to you. . . .You taught me that there is no substitute for hard work, and I am not afraid of it. . . . You taught me to be polite and respectful and to fight for what I believe is right, as you did when they were trying to integrate those of us with special problems into a 'normal' school room situation. You made them aware that all of us have special needs in education, and you were certainly the perfect answer to mine". (1978)

* * *

When Andrea graduated from St. John Fisher College in Rochester, N.Y. in 1983 with a Bachelor's degree in Communications and Journalism, my graduation gift to her was a copy of *The Book of Psalms*. She worked from home as a free lance writer. During this time, she also served voluntarily as Vice President of the Rochester Center for Independent Living, using her writing skills to obtain grants for the agency.

She wrote to me about it saying, "Although it is happening slowly, I'm beginning to hold my own in Rochester's media family. Several of my friends from Fisher are now contacts I work with on a regular basis and it's a nice feeling to be able to trade favors and make recommendations to each other. It is such a blessing to know that dreams we had when we were younger are now within our reach and in some cases are coming true And I agree with you that children live what they learn. " (1989)

"I was elected to the Rochester Center for Independent Living Board of Directors and am the chairperson of the Legislative and Advocacy Committee." (1989)

* * *

Andrea continued her education at Syracuse University, receiving her Masters in Social Work in December, 1994, and her C.S.W. from the State of New York in June of 1995.

"I've begun pursuing a Master's degree in Social Work at Syracuse University. I'm very excited about this new path. I love writing and I believe that it is the foundation for effective communication, but it's a very solitary profession with an unfortunate element that includes self-imposed exile. I will be specializing in a family mental health concentration — working specifically with women and parents of children with disabilities.

"One thing that disturbs me greatly are theories that regard the development of children with disabilities as deviant from 'normal.' I believe that these children develop according to a healthy logic of their own if, just like able-bodied children, they are in an optimal environment. I think this is an area that merits much more study." (1991)

* * *

Later, she wrote to me again: "I am in the middle of my second and final clinical rotation and hope to have my Master's degree in Social Work next December. Currently I work in an outpatient psychiatric clinic at Strong Memorial Hospital as a primary therapist. I find the work challenging, rewarding and emotionally draining. I also travel, along with several of my classmates, to Syracuse University for weekly classes. I'm still in awe that I actually am allowed to sit in these lectures and learn all of this wonderful stuff!

"Last year I worked as a social worker on a multidisciplinary team in the Fairport School District at the elementary level, including a Special Ed classroom. I also worked at the high school as part of a transition team, preparing students with special needs for future education or vocational placement. I have never felt so wonderful about the work I was doing. The Director of Pupil Services has asked me to return to the district when I complete my degree. I have always known, ever since I was blessed enough to learn from you, that I wanted to work in an academic environment. I think I have finally found my life's calling and now I can't wait to begin!" (1993)

* * *

Andrea was working as an elementary school social worker up to the time of her last illness when she wrote to me: "I have begun working as a school social worker in the Fairport District. I wish 'my' children could have the guidance of your wisdom and gentle grace. I am finding the work challenging, wonderful and painful." (1994)

Andrea died in February, 1999.

* * *

Ann Kurz graduated from Trinity College in Washington, D.C. with a B.A. in Sociology in 1983, and earned a Masters degree in Computers in Education from the University of Rochester in 1986. She now works for Wegmans Food Markets as a marketing analyst at the corporate level.

She sits on the Rochester Cerebral Palsy Board of Directors, volunteers for Rochester's United Way and is active in both her church and her community.

She and Andrea Levy were dear friends in elementary school for three years in the ungraded 4th, 5th and 6th grades at Adlai E. Stevenson School (#29) in Rochester. She recalls that she and Andrea went their separate ways when Ann left in the middle of 6th grade to go for intensive therapy in Valhalla, N.Y.

She wrote: "When I returned a year later, mainstreaming special education children had begun and I was mainstreamed into my school district while Andrea was mainstreamed across town into her school district. Although our daily friendship ended we kept in touch at Christmas time with cards and year-end letters.

"Andrea had a form of muscular dystrophy, I believe. We didn't really ask one another what our disabilities were. I guess that it didn't matter; we were too busy being kids and friends!

"Miss Remis had Andrea and I keep daily journals, which I still have. They are typewritten because I could hardly write and Andrea tired quickly."

* * *

From Andrea Levy's diary, December 15, 1971. "On my way home yesterday, I saw a sign SOCKAWAYABUCKADAY. This means to put a dollar in the bank each day. The bus driver told me it's one big word. If a multi-millionaire is a person who has many millions, then SOCKAWAYABUCKADAY must be a multi-compound word.

* * *

From Ann Kurz's diary, January 5, 1973: "Today is the last day Ann will be writing in her diary here, at school #29. Monday the eighth she is going to Blythedale for six months. Someone has to come in with a smile. Blythedale is near New York City. You have to cross the Hudson River. It's in Valhalla. Ann is going to miss all her friends and her family in Rochester. In Blythedale they have a public phone in the building. Ann is going to call her family every Friday. Here is what Ann dials: 0-716-xxx-xxxx. You dial zero if you want the people you are calling to pay the bill. You dial one if you are paying the bill. Ann's mother taught her this."

* * *

Ann Kurz also wrote a short paragraph about the Spanish class that was published in *The Bugle,* Public School #29's school newspaper. She later told me that the importance of learning Spanish impressed her so much that her minor at Trinity College was Spanish.

* * *

Many years ago I read a poem by Clare Tree Major, who was a popular writer in the 1930's. Today, I can find no reference in print or on the Internet to her or her poetry. But I know this poem "by heart" because it eloquently expresses all that I have gained from my 29 years of teaching children with disabilities:

Would you set your name among the stars?
Then write it large upon the hearts of children.
They will remember.

Have you visions of a finer, happier world?
Tell the children, they will build it for you.
Have you a word of hope for poor, blind, stumbling human kind?
Give it not to intelligent, blundering man.
Give it to the children.
In their clear, untroubled minds
It will reflect itself a thousandfold.
And someday paint itself upon the mountain tops.

Somewhere a Lincoln plays and listens and watches
        with bewildered eye
This strange procession of mild-mannered souls.
Have you a ray of light to offer? Then give it.
And it will help to light the world to freedom and to joy.

Anne I. Remis, December 2003

101